T0368665

Four Wheels For Two Legs

Sheer Determination No Matter What

Order this book online at www.trafford.com
or email orders@trafford.com

Most Trafford titles are also available at major online book retailers.

© Copyright 2004 Alison A. McGovern.
All rights reserved. No part of this publication may be reproduced, stored in a retrieval system, or transmitted, in any form or by
any means, electronic, mechanical, photocopying, recording, or otherwise, without the written prior permission of the author.

Print information available on the last page.

ISBN: 978-1-4120-2683-3 (sc)

Because of the dynamic nature of the Internet, any web addresses or links contained in this book may have changed
since publication and may no longer be valid. The views expressed in this work are solely those of the author and do
not necessarily reflect the views of the publisher, and the publisher hereby disclaims any responsibility for them.

Any people depicted in stock imagery provided by Getty Images are models, and
such images are being used for illustrative purposes only.
Certain stock imagery © Getty Images.

Trafford rev. 02/29/2020

 www.trafford.com

North America & international
toll-free: 1 888 232 4444 (USA & Canada)
fax: 812 355 4082

ACKNOWLEDGEMENTS

Special thanks must go to:-

The Evening Herald Newspaper – Plymouth Devon
Bernard White/The Cornish Guardian Newspaper
The Big Sheep – Bideford Devon
The Cambridge Evening News Newspaper
Mary Wareham
SKYCITY Auckland Sky Tower – New Zealand

Back Cover Photograph:
Alison in New Zealand with her Uncle David, Aunty Helen,
twin sister Julia, Grandpa Kerr, Dad, Nana Kerr and brother Peter -
taken during Christmas 1969.

Front Cover Photograph:
Alison with her Mum in King Street, Cambridge, England –
taken on Monday 16th June 2003.

THIS BOOK IS DEDICATED
TO MUM &DAD

—

WHO GAVE ME LIFE
IN THE FIRST PLACE

ALISON & JULIA

CHAPTER:-

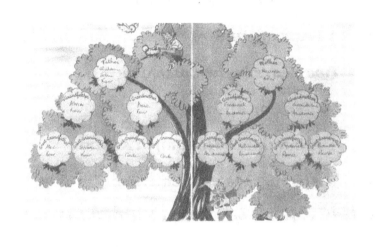

CHAPTER ONE

EARLY CHILDHOOD MEMORIES

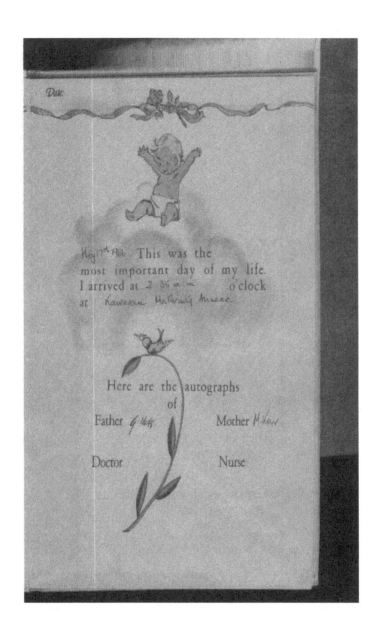

Date

May 17th 1966. This was the most important day of my life. I arrived at 2:36 a.m. o'clock at Kawerau Maternity Annexe

Here are the autographs
of

Father *G. Hoff*   Mother *M. Hoff*

Doctor   Nurse

"Goodbye Ali, see you on Friday."

Ever since my early childhood days, that sentence has sat at the back of my mind. For the first ten years of my life I was brought up in New Zealand along with my twin sister, Julia, and our older brother, Peter.

You are probably saying to yourself now – "Why should a sentence like that remain at the back of her mind?" The reason being is because I was born with a disability called Cerebral Palsy. Living with such a disability meant spending a lot of time away from home, as my parents thought it would be best for me to attend special units and schools for handicapped children.

It is here where that opening sentence applies. At a very young age I was sent to a Cerebral Palsy Unit in Rotorua, where I stayed during the week, and returned home at the weekend.

Cerebral Palsy, in my case, was caused through lack of oxygen at birth. Cerebral means, 'of the brain, intellectual' and Palsy means, 'paralysis with involuntary tremors.' Unfortunately all my limbs are affected – I am very stiff and my mobility is severely restricted. Incidentally, Julia and I were very eager to join the big wide world, because we were ten weeks premature. At birth I weighed a very delicate 3lbs 2ozs!! I spent the first nine weeks of my life in Whakatane Hospital. I was then discharged from hospital weighing 6lbs, 1oz.

An extract from my Baby Book reads:-

"In my first year I had a lot of brand new and exciting experiences which I had better make a note of here, lest I forget them"; then Mum wrote the following:-

"Rolled over at beginning of '67. Sits with support for longer periods and getting more control over head – also sits in the "walkabout" for short periods and is able to go in the pushchair – gone forward at 18 months.

14.1.68. Can now sit in "walkabout" and move it for longer periods. Sits in car seat now as from 12.1.68. Enjoying life more now although still cries a lot, probably still frustrated. Very sweet little thing really. Visited chiropractor in Feb. and March – much happier, sits up better but still not unsupported. Legs don't cross now – less rigidity, holding head better. Taking more interest and has occasional "tangles" with Julia – pulls her hair etc. Sits up straight in the pushchair as from March 1st.

Visited Dr. Watson in Hamilton June 24th. Referred to CPU in Rotorua – commenced LUCIDRIL – effects: - happier – brighter – more control – trying to crawl – sitting in pegstool unsupported. Visited by CPU therapists and Crippled Children's Society."

My memories of life in New Zealand are extremely vague. I do remember though, very consciously, my days at Carlson C.P. School. That was a special school in Auckland which catered for children with cerebral palsy. It was a non-residential school, so I was obviously able to go home in the evening which I thought was absolutely fabulous as I was able to spend time with Julia and Pete. I also felt part of the family.

CARLSON SCHOOL FOR CEREBRAL PALSY

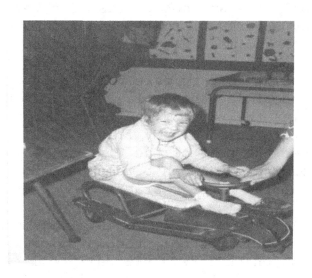

ALISON AT CARLSON SCHOOL

Julia and I were Brownies. We even went on a couple of Brownie camps together. I shall never forget the time when I offered to do the washing-up - what a disaster that was! Instead of washing the dishes, I ended up washing the floor, as I accidentally (no, not on purpose!) knocked the bowl full of hot water and dirty dishes on to the floor. So, instead of me doing the dishes, everybody else did them

from then on because they didn't want
to have to mop the floor as well as
wash the dishes!!

**PETE WITH HIS TWIN SISTERS
ALISON AND JULIA**

Returning to the subject of Carlson
School, the atmosphere was of a very
happy nature. I really enjoyed my time
there, and made plenty of friends. My
happiest memory about Carlson School
was being able to take part in the
Wizard of Oz school play. My role was
to play the part of the Lion, who was
full of courage!! My friend Philip
played the part of the Tin Man!!
Unfortunately I can't remember who
played the other characters.

Despite Carlson School being known
as a special school, the level of
education there was virtually nil. We
were taught the extreme basics.
Physiotherapy and Occupational therapy
took priority over Maths and English.
I even had a few sessions of speech
therapy. Don't for heaven sake ask me
why, as fortunately I don't have any
problems communicating!

I didn't enjoy physiotherapy very
much at all - in fact, I hated it at
times, especially when the
physiotherapists would undress me down
to my vest and pants so that they could
have a closer look at my limbs. They

12

did teach me how to use a special
walking frame though and I loved that –
it was much better than having to rely
on a wheelchair all the time.

In order to get to and from school,
I travelled by taxi – my fares I think,
were paid for by the local authority.
I shall always remember my taxi driver
with great affection. He was a very
kind and pleasant Chinese or Japanese
man – I was never quite sure which!
His name was Mr Fong.

**THE KERR FAMILY HOME
18 ANARAHI PLACE
AUCKLAND NEW ZEALAND**

Unfortunately my days at Carlson
School were soon to come to an abrupt
end. Mum became terribly homesick for
England, as that is where she was born
and she desperately wanted to live
there again.

In May 1976 we all emigrated to
England to begin our new way of life.

One thing which will always remain
in my mind about leaving New Zealand

was seeing all our possessions, well
perhaps not all, but quite a few, being
gradually packed up in tea-chests or
sold. Even now, as I am typing, I can
see in my mind, Mum and Dad's bed going
down the road on a trailer! Our cat
went to live with Philip and his
family.

It took us several months to settle
down to our new way of life. To begin
with we had to recover from an
extremely long flight from Auckland to
London Heathrow. To break the journey,
we spent forty-eight hours in
Singapore. Our accommodation was the
Holiday Inn Hotel - that was certainly
a very posh place. I must say how
impressed I was with the hotel, but I
wasn't at all impressed with the
wheelchair that the hotel staff very
kindly lent me - it was far too big,
and I felt extremely lost in it!

During our short time in Singapore
Mum and Dad bought me an electric
typewriter. I was absolutely over the
moon because given the opportunity, I
love doing typing. Julia and Pete were
treated to something nice as well -
they couldn't be left out, but I can't
remember what Mum and Dad bought them.

**ALISON'S SMITH CORONA
ELECTRIC TYPEWRITER**

When we arrived at London Heathrow, Mum was absolutely delighted to know that she was back on English soil again. Her brother and sister-in-law, Uncle Gerald and Aunty Eileen were at the airport to meet us.

Having just arrived in England, we didn't have anywhere to live. We stayed with Uncle Gerald and Aunty Eileen for a little while but unfortunately had to leave due to a family disagreement.

For the following six months our relations Sue and Vic, said that we could stay with them. They lived in St. Budeaux, Plymouth - not far from the Tamar Bridge, the divider between Devon and Cornwall. After staying with Sue and Vic, we lived in a caravan followed by a cottage, then a caravan again! The caravan was to be our home for several weeks until Mum and Dad managed to save enough money for a deposit towards a two bedroom starter home.

Life in the caravan was very uncomfortable and frustrating for me at times. Access for getting me in and out was quite difficult due to steps being outside the door instead of a ramp. There weren't any toilet facilities in the caravan, they were completely separate, (a few minutes walk away) and unfortunately for me, there wasn't a toilet which had been adapted for handicapped people to use. If I needed to answer the call of nature, Mum or Dad would sit me on a potty on the floor in the caravan, and that was where I had to do my business - whatever the case may be. Dad took me into the gents loos once or twice to

save me sitting on the potty - I was
extremely grateful to him for that, as
having just turned ten years of age, I
obviously had feelings and I felt
extremely down-graded and embarrassed
about having to do my business on a
potty. After all, lets face it, I'm a
human being, and I'm entitled to
privacy, especially when going to the
toilet.

   Just when I thought I'd escaped from
being sent away from home (because Mum
and Dad warned me when we were still in
New Zealand that I might be going to a
boarding school in England) I was told
that I was to attend a special school
in Ivybridge, Devon - called Dame
Hannah Rogers School. I was to board
there on a fortnightly basis, spending
alternate weekends at home.

**ALISON – ON THE DAY I BECAME A PUPIL AT
DAME HANNAH ROGERS SCHOOL –
"I WAS YET TO BE ISSUED WITH MY RED TIE!!"**

   At first I found being away from
home extremely hard to accept. I felt
very very insecure mainly because I was
in a completely different country and
everything was new to me. I was also

missing all my friends at Carlson
School in Auckland. A couple of
letters from my friends read:-

Carlson School
261 St. Andrews Road
Three Kings
Auckland
New Zealand

18.6.76

Dear Alison,

I hope you like your new school in England.

I have a dog now and he can eat meat. We just call him
Doggy.

I hope you are feeling well.

Love from

Joanna

Carlson School
261 St. Andrews Road

25.6.76

Dear Alison,

I miss you.

I learn spelling every day. Today we had a test and I got
all my words right.

Love from Scott   xxxxxxxxxxoooooxxooo

A letter from my school teacher Mrs
Snow, read:-

Carlson School for
Cerebral Palsy
261 St. Andrews Road
Three Kings

23rd June 1976

Dear Alison,

We were all very excited to find your lovely postcard
in the mail, written in your own writing. All the children
are writing letters to you, but we thought it would be
better to send these off. We hope you have settled in well
and are happy at your new school. Often we think of you
sleeping while we are working at school and wonder if
you think the same about us.

We have some news that we are all excited about.
Mr Snow and I are leaving for England next week. We are
going by ship to New Orleans. From there we will be
flying to Houston in Texas, Philadelphia in Pennsylvania,
then Washington before flying to England on 31st July.

Mr Snow and I are both looking forward to seeing
you and all your family at sometime during August. I
shall be writing to your mother too.

There will be much to tell you when we see you, and
a great many questions to ask you. I'm sure you have
made many new friends, but your old ones think of you
often.

I thought my letter would be ready to send with the
first set of letters, but other things had to be done. Never
mind, I trust it finds you well.

Yours sincerely

Peg Snow

Sure enough, I did see Peg Snow and it was absolutely wonderful. My only regret is that I did not keep in touch with her.

"Peg, if you should ever happen to read this book, I would very much like to give you this message. Thank you for giving me such a happy time during my days at Carlson School as they were thoroughly enjoyable, and I apologise sincerely for not keeping in touch with you. Perhaps one day, we may be reunited!"

I shall always remember the first time I was allowed to go home for the weekend from Dame Hannah Rogers School! We were driving on the A38 dual carriageway from Ivybridge towards Plymouth, when I said very strongly to Mum and Dad, "I am **NOT** going back to that place because I am put to bed at six thirty every night." I was certainly not the world's happiest person!! Whatever next, first of all I have to do my business sitting on a potty. I'm then sent to a place where I'm put to bed at six thirty every night.

Unfortunately I did have to return, and when I saw the school in the distance, I would burst into tears and literally plead to Mum and Dad to take me home again as I just could not bear the thought of them saying goodbye, and leaving me behind. I thought, "What on earth have I done to deserve this?"

I wasn't the only child who felt like that. Some children would cry themselves to sleep. My friend Beverley would turn absolutely hysterical!

**DAME HANNAH ROGERS SCHOOL
IVYBRIDGE DEVON**

CHAPTER TWO

A TASTE OF FAME

1415 PLYMOUTH YBS 13

ALISON KERR SALTRAM HOUSE PLYMPTON PLYMOUTH

SLEEP WELL PRINCESS

SWEET DREAMS

PRINCE CHARMING

To be honest I never really got over my homesickness during my time at Dame Hannah Rogers School, but as time went by it became less painful when I was faced with the uncomfortable situation of having to say "goodbye" to my family.

After all, I was a pupil at Dame Hannah's for six years (1976 – 1982) which is quite a big chunk out of my life, and I felt that I had to try and make the most of those precious years – do my best with my education and physiotherapy, and enjoy myself at the same time!

A postcard postmarked 21st June 1976 with a photo of the Barbican, Plymouth on the front, received from Mum, Dad, Pete and Julia, read:-

Dear Ali,

We drove to the Barbican after we left you yesterday. Tell Dixie that we left your little bag which she made at home, and that your name tapes have arrived. We are not going to London this week – probably next week.

We will see you on Saturday for the Sports Day, so till then, be happy and lots of love from us all.

Mum, Dad, Pete & Julia   xxxxx

The biggest memory that my family and I will always have regarding the 1976 Dame Hannah Rogers School Sports Day, is that Dad won a black and white portable television in the raffle. Beverley Shannon's Dad, Eddie, was chairing the raffle and his words were something like, "First Prize – a portable black and white television. The winner is ……………… GRAHAM KERR."

**ALISON AT DAME HANNAH ROGERS SCHOOL
SPORTS DAY – 1976
"FIRST PERSON TO BITE THE BUN OFF THE STRING
AND EAT IT!!!!!!"**

Dad was really taken by surprise –
he couldn't believe his luck!!

Following Dad's lucky win, I
received the following letters:-

3 Kinterbury Tce
Bull Point
St Budeaux
Plymouth

Dear Ali

How are you? We are alright it is very hot today don't you
think? How much money did you get at the fair? Has Shep barked
yet? We haven't got the T.V. yet. That is all I can think of for now
so Good Bye.

Love From Peter.

30.6.76

Dear Ali,

Hi! How are you these days? Have you worn out those
new shoes yet?

I THINK YOU SAID YOU WANTED ME TO PRINT THE
LETTER TO YOU. I'VE JUST REMEMBERED.

WE HAD A LOVELY DAY AT YOUR SPORTS.
WEREN'T WE LUCKY TO WIN A T.V. SET IN THE RAFFLE.

IT IS STILL VERY HOT ISN'T IT, BUT DAD AND I
WON'T GO IN FOR A SWIM AS THE WATER IS SO COLD
THAT IT MAKES OUR FEET AND LEGS ACHE TOO MUCH,
AND THAT'S NOT TOO GOOD. PETER AND JULIA ARE
GRADUALLY GETTING USED TO THE SEA. IT'S CALLED
THE ENGLISH CHANNEL AROUND HERE. DID YOU
KNOW THAT? PERHAPS MISS HUSKISSON COULD SHOW
YOU ON A MAP ONE DAY. WE THOUGHT THE POM-POM
YOU ARE MAKING WITH THE WOOL WAS LOVELY.
THERE ARE SOME VERY CLEVER CHILDREN AT YOUR
SCHOOL.

WE HAD A LETTER FROM GRAN AND GRAMPA AND THEY SEND THEIR LOVE TO YOU AND THEY MISS TAKING YOU FOR WALKS.

SUSAN, VIC AND JULIE ENJOYED THEMSELVES AT PENRYN WITH UNCLE ALEC, AUNTY ROMA AND BRANDY THE DOG. THEY ALL SEND THEIR LOVE TO YOU.

PETER HAS BEEN DOING EXAMS AT HIS SCHOOL, AND HE GOT 83 MARKS OUT OF 100 FOR MATHS, SO THAT WAS VERY CLEVER OF HIM.

JULIA LINED UP WITH HER SCHOOL YESTERDAY TO WATCH PRINCESS ALEXANDRA OPEN A SPECIAL HOUSE. WE SAW HER WITH HER HUSBAND ANGUS OGILVY IN NEW ZEALAND. DO YOU REMEMBER?

ARE YOU ENJOYING YOUR BATHS AND SHAMPOOS? STILL HAVING GOOD FOOD? WE ARE HAVING FISH FINGERS FOR TEA TONIGHT. I DON'T LIKE GOING SHOPPING VERY MUCH AS THE SUPERMARKETS ARE TOO CROWDED. NOT LIKE GUBAYS!

HOW IS YOUR NEW SUN HAT? WE HOPE THAT IT HAS BLOWN AWAY YET! HAVE YOU GOT ENOUGH CLOTHES TO WEAR? WE DO HOPE SO. WE MIGHT BE ABLE TO MANAGE SOMETHING ELSE ONE OF THESE DAYS.

SEE YOU ON THE 9TH. WE ALL SEND OUR LOVE TO YOU. TAKE CARE & BE HAPPY ALLY-WALLY! LOVE FROM MUM, DAD, PETE & JULIA   XXXX

ALISON READY FOR A WALK "AROUND THE BLOCK" WITH HER GRAN AND GRANDPA & MICKY THE DOG

GRAN AND GRANDPA'S BUNGALOW
MABE BURNTHOUSE NEAR PENRYN CORNWALL

ALISON LAPPING UP THE ENGLISH SUNSHINE

**ALISON ENJOYING A STROLL
IN LOOE CORNWALL**

**ALISON AND AN EXTREMELY FRIENDLY
DARTMOOR PONY!**

A postcard from Mum and Dad,
postmarked London - displaying several
famous landmarks of London on the
front, read:-

Dear Alice,

How are you in all this hot weather? We (mum and
dad) came up to London today to fetch all our goodies. We

shall be up this way again next week to see Uncle Geoffrey-effry. Hope school is going ok for you. We got our new TV the other day and it is a very jazzy one. Love from
Mum and Dad xx.

Incidentally, Shep, the dog which Pete mentioned in his letter to me, I think belonged to the Headmistress, Miss Sutcliffe, as he was always sitting outside her office. Shep was never a naughty dog though!!

It was only a matter of weeks after I became a pupil at Dame Hannah Rogers School, that Miss Sutcliffe retired, and Shep must have gone into retirement as well, because sadly, from then on I cannot recall Shep sitting outside the office anymore.

Following Miss Sutcliffe's retirement, Mr Yiend was asked to act as Headmaster until Mr Huxtable was appointed in the late 1970's.

My school report for Summer Term 1978, signed by Mr Huxtable, as Headmaster, read:-

DAME HANNAH ROGERS SCHOOL
Approved by the Department of Education and Science for
CHILDREN WITH CEREBRAL PALSY AND OTHER PHYSICAL HANDICAP
Affiliated to The Spastics Society

IVYBRIDGE, DEVON

NAME: Alison Kerr   AGE: 13yrs 7mths

<u>SUMMER TERM 1978</u>

<u>General Remarks</u>:

Alison takes great pride in her work and maintains a consistently high standard in all her subjects. She is thoughtful in all that she does, and she is always reliable. Her good manners and conscientious behaviour give such pleasure and set a good example to us all. She also has a good sense of humour.

<u>Music</u> She has enjoyed playing simple duets this term and of course she has persisted with these pieces until she reached her own high standard. She has been a good example to others in her diligent music practice.

<u>Discovery</u> Of herself Alison does not initiate ideas and interests, but when presented with them she produces good, neat follow-up work. Her retention and recall of facts are good, as is her concentration, also her imaginative and dramatic powers are developing most satisfactorily.

R.A.J. Lovell

Physiotherapy Report:

The question of surgery has been postponed until Alison is older. She continues to practice walking with tripods and enjoys walking on the arm of one person which is useful.

It is important that Alison has regular chiropody.

E. M. Alexander

Social Development:

Alison has been happy to resume horse riding lessons now the evenings are light, and took part in a Gymkhana for Disabled Riders, winning several events.

She attended the Guides' Camp in Surrey during the half-term holiday, and had a wonderful time despite the unseasonable weather.

Alison is popular with the other children, and has several close friends, but this sometimes leads to someone doing something for her which she is quite able to do for herself. She needs no help in dressing and undressing, apart from fastening her shoes, and with some supervision can get in and out of the bath.

D M Dixon

Headmaster's Comments:

Alison sets a good example to others – she puts much effort into her life and gets a great deal of satisfaction from her achievements.

R.D. Huxtable
Headmaster

PRINCESS ANNE

**ALISON RIDING MOTHY
WITH HER HELPERS AT THE
RIDING FOR THE DISABLED GYMKHANA
ATTENDED BY PRINCESS ANNE**

Horse riding gave me immense enjoyment and pleasure. Every Tuesday evening in the summer time, I was taken by Miss Barnacle, who was the Chairman for the Riding for the Disabled Association South Dartmoor Group, to a Riding for the Disabled Association Riding School, at Yelverton on Dartmoor, for lessons.

I enjoyed every aspect of riding, and it was a great feeling to be free of my wheelchair. To find a hat that fitted my head was quite a challenge! When my horse, quite often Bumble, switched up a gear to the trotting mode, I would not only develop a fit of the giggles, but would also either lose my hat altogether, or it would fall down over my eyes so I obviously couldn't see where on earth I was going!!

As a group we would frequently go riding across Dartmoor. I can remember one occasion - my horse decided to suddenly put his head down to eat grass, and because I wasn't concentrating, I ended up going straight over the horse's head, landing on the grass - just missing a cowpat!! By the way, not surprisingly, my hat didn't protect me at all!!!

It was a real honour to meet Princess Anne when I took part in a gymkhana at which she was present. I thought Princess Anne was very pleasant and very down to earth.

Because I enjoyed horse riding so much I decided to compile a 'horsy' scrapbook, and for my effort I was awarded a Riding for the Disabled Handbook on behalf of the South Dartmoor Group. Miss Barnacle's letter read:-

66 Beaumaris Road,
Hartley Vale,
Plymouth.

June '79

Dear Alison,

The Committee of the South Dartmoor Group Riding for the Disabled Association would like to congratulate you on your excellent scrapbook. What a great deal of work you must have put into it. I have great pleasure on their behalf of awarding you this prize for a very good effort.

Josephine Barnacle

N.J. Barnacle.
Chairman
South Dartmoor Group

———————————

**ALISON RIDING HER FAVOURITE HORSE BUMBLE –
"RIDING BUMBLE BROUGHT ME MY FIRST CLAIM TO
FAME AS WE WERE BOTH FEATURED ON
BBC SPOTLIGHT SOUTH WEST"**

**ALISON DAD AND BEST SCHOOL FRIEND
HILARY HERRINGTON**

I wasn't the only member of our
family who spent time away from home.
Dad spent a fair amount of time away
from home as well, due to him being a
merchant seaman.

Dad would sometimes be away at sea
for months at a time, especially if he
was doing deep-sea trips which involved
sailing to different ports throughout
the world.

Saying "goodbye" to Dad at the
railway station or airport was
extremely difficult for me. A few
minutes before having to say that
dreaded word, a huge lump would develop
in my throat – and no matter how hard I
tried, I just could not hold back the
tears.

Welcoming Dad back home again was
a completely different story – I felt
like the happiest person in the world.
I would sometimes cry tears of joy!

**PETE AND ALISON
ON BOARD ONE OF DAD'S SHIPS
"DON'T I JUST LOOK THE PART!!!"**

One letter from Dad read:-

AT SEA 3 DAYS FROM SINGAPORE

25th April 1979.

My Dearest Alice,

I was very pleased to get your letters, especially the big one, I really thought it was a letter from the Company office in London. I am so glad you all came up to Cardiff when we were there, it was an interesting couple of days for you all, but the train ride home wasn't as good as the one coming up was it? However I'll be back home again with you all soon, for about 3 months this time.

We have travelled about 12,000 miles so far this time & its been quite a long trip, 2 months since we left Amsterdam.

It was quite interesting when we reached Argentina & left the open sea to go up a narrow river which was only about four times as wide as the ship. It was like being in the jungle with lots of thick bush & trees on both sides. Occasionally there was a little landing jutting out & in among the bushes a little house on stilts, & then some children & a few chooks would come running & the boys & girls would yell out & wave to the ship. There are all sorts of large moths and creeping beetles on the ship at night. When we got to the port it was quite big & we had to anchor for a couple of days before there was room for us to go alongside to load. While we were at anchor we had hoses squirting water on the anchor chains all the time to stop, (pull the bed clothes over your head now) poisonous sea snakes from getting up the chain & on to the ship, just imagine them coming into your bedroom at night!

We are many miles from there now & out in the lovely warm (32oC) Indian Ocean. We called at Durban to get this great ocean greyhound a drink, 1500 tons of heavy oil & as it drinks 40 ton per day we already have used a quarter of it.

When we stopped at Durban we also loaded quite a lot of food to keep us fuelled up too, & among all the goodies was paw paw, or do you remember when we went to Hawaii it was called Papaya, it is an orange fruit & tastes beautiful, we have plenty of it to last us.

Nobody knows yet where we will be off to after Singapore, perhaps to Indonesia to load more timber & back to Britain, perhaps to NZ?

I do hope you have had some better weather in England since I left as it was a long winter wasn't it? Have you been in the new swimming pool yet? I have had a few swims in our one on here.

I'll get the Chief Engineer & his wife to take this letter back & post it for me, they live just up the road in Teignmouth & have been on here since the port before Cardiff, which was Valencia in Spain. They are going home for a few days to get things sorted out & then they are off to their daughter's place in Vancouver, Canada for about 6 weeks holiday.

I will get some cards in Singapore & send them off to you all & will look for some cheap tapes.

I was very pleased with Pete having passed his exams & was delighted to hear from you that he will be a prefect as he never said so himself.

It is 7.30 pm now my baby & I'm off to work very shortly so I must leave you for the time.

Once again Alice, thank you for all your lovely letters, they were most welcome.

Bye for now, see you soon, lots of love to you from Dad

xxxxxxxx

"A very interesting and educational letter Dad, thank you very much. I am pleased to say that I didn't have nightmares about the sea snakes coiling themselves around the anchor chain in order to board your ship - oooh, it doesn't bear thinking about - what an awful thought!! Thank **you** also for all your letters and postcards which you sent me, during your long periods of time away at sea - they were greatly appreciated."

Following my appearance with Bumble on BBC Spotlight South West, my claim to fame was not only when I met Julian Orchard and Norman Wisdom at the Palace Theatre in Plymouth, but also when I spent the night sleeping in a four poster bed at Saltram House, Plympton, Plymouth, as a guest of the National Trust.

JULIAN ORCHARD

I was absolutely delighted to
receive this letter from Julian
Orchard:-

THE NEW PALACE THEATRE
PLYMOUTH.

Jan. 26th 1979.

Dear Alison,

Thank you so much for your lovely letter. It was fun
meeting you outside the stage door after the show.

I am sorry that we didn't have more time to talk, but we
have to do the show twice some days, and it takes me quite a
long time to turn myself into an ugly sister.

The pretend car chase is fun, I'm glad you liked it. We
practiced the pantomime for about ten days before we
actually opened to the public. We have to learn all the words,
and where we are supposed to stand, as well as the songs,
and dances, so we have to work very hard. We call this our
rehearsals.

The people who come to the pantomime seem to be
very friendly, and so its like a big party all the time.

I hope you will always enjoy the theatre, and come and
see the shows at the Palace Theatre.

I would like to wish you a very happy new year, and I
must tell you that I think you write beautifully.

Yours with all my best wishes,

Julian Orchard

JULIAN ORCHARD

P.S. I'm sending you a photograph with my autograph on it.
I hope you like it.

"I loved your signed photograph
Julian – thank you very very much."

NORMAN WISDOM

"Thank you very much Norman for your
signed photograph as well."

A further school report read:-

DAME HANNAH ROGERS SCHOOL

Approved by the Department of Education and Science for children with cerebral palsy and other physical handicap
Affiliated to The Spastics Society

IVYBRIDGE, DEVON

NAME: Alison Kerr

REPORT FOR TERM ENDING: 22 July 1980

AGE: 14.2

EDUCATIONAL ATTAINMENT:

Alison is painstakingly careful and conscientious about her work. She is logical and precise and the next thing to aim for is a greater fluency of style in her writing.

She is making slow but steady progress with mathematics, the present aim being more confidence in dealing with decimals and multiplying and dividing by ten.

Luckily she is a competent reader, and the wideness of her taste in literature is much to be encouraged. I hope the speed of her reading will increase; this would be an advantage to her, and I hope to help her in this direction next term.

Alison's charming manners and her determination are acknowledged throughout the school.

PHYSIOTHERAPIST'S REPORT:

Alison has matured over the year and works hard during treatment sessions.

She was able to participate in the Ten Tors Special Event this year and gained a Bronze medal on completion of the 6½ mile road route which she did in her wheelchair. During the training period she showed great tenacity of purpose and worked to the top of her potential. Regular foot care is necessary.

Swimming is enjoyed very much. Alison is always happy and polite and is very welcome in the department.

E.M. Alexander.

SOCIAL DEVELOPMENT:

Alison has many friends and is well liked by children and staff. She has had a very good year of steady progress. She is always pleasant, and willing to help others at all times, Alison is kind and considerate.

Her determined nature has resulted in her being able to get herself in and out of the bath. She is now practicing to wash her own hair, and is doing very well.

Alison is a keen Guide, and also enjoys her visits to PHAB every Wednesday. She is always busy at the weekends and pleased to join in with most activities.

Alison has learnt to man the school telephone, and is efficient in answering and taking messages.

HEADMASTER'S REMARKS:

The high standards which Alison sets for herself inspire others to greater effort.

My love for Saltram House arose
during a school class visit to the
National Trust property in October
1979. As my classmates, our teacher,
(Tony Duncan) and I were being guided
around the Great Kitchen and House, I
had visions in my mind of life in grand
houses during days gone by.

When I saw the four-poster beds, I
was so impressed by them I said to Tony
Duncan, "Do you think one day it would
be possible for me to spend a night
sleeping here in a four-poster bed?"

Tony's reply was, "Why don't you
write a letter to Jim'll Fix It and ask
him if he can fix it for you."

Sadly, I didn't receive a reply from
Jim. I was obviously very
disappointed. Several months passed
by, then I noticed a poster displayed
on the school notice-board which read:-

"TIM'LL FIX IT

HAVE YOU GOT ANYTHING YOU WOULD REALLY LIKE ME TO FIX FOR YOU?"

After reading Tim's notice, I
thought to myself, "Yes, I have," so I
wrote a letter to Tim. A few more
months passed by. I then received a
message from Tim saying that he could
fix it for me. I was absolutely
thrilled to bits - to say the least!

On 21st October 1980, a photographer
from the Ivybridge Gazette came to
school to take photos of me. I didn't

know he was coming until Mrs Dyke, the
secretary, came into my classroom and
asked Mr Yiend if the photographer
could take photos of me. The article
in the Ivybridge Gazette read:-

Alison set for stately kip

TO spend a night in a four-poster bed in a beautiful
old house must appeal to many a romantic nature, but it
is a dream come true for 14 year old Alison Kerr.

She has been picked by Ivybridge Round Table as
the next in line for the Tim'll Fix It project.

Alison, a pupil at Dame Hannah Rogers School,
wrote to Tim Hardwick, Table community services
chairman, who recently arranged for two boys to visit a
submarine.

She saw his posters advertising the Fix It service, on
similar lines to the one run by television personality,
Jimmy Savile, and decided she would like to stay the
night at Saltram House.

Her teacher Mr Tony Duncan told the Gazette; "In
October last year I took my class to Saltram and we had a
good look round."

"Alison was so struck by the house. She wrote to
Jim'll Fix It, but got no reply, then she heard about the
Round Table scheme and applied to them."

"We have been joking with her that the house is
haunted, but she knows it is a leg pull."

Tim Hardwick was surprised it could all be
arranged. "The National Trust was very good about it
and will provide supper, a four-poster bed and breakfast
in the morning."

Jean Harris, of the National Trust said they were pleased to help.

"Alison will have a supper, where it is hoped her brother and sister can come too. She will stay the night, with her mother next door in what used to be the maid's room. And then breakfast will be brought to her in bed by a maid and butler."

Alison said she is very much looking forward to the visit, which is due to take place next week.

My extremely enjoyable "stately kip" took place on Monday, 27th October 1980 – the memories of which will remain with me for the rest of my life.

May I take this opportunity to say, from the bottom of my heart, a **BIG** thank you to everyone who helped to make my stay at Saltram so enjoyable and memorable. I felt highly privileged. It was an absolutely wonderful experience.

"THANK YOU ALL VERY VERY MUCH INDEED."

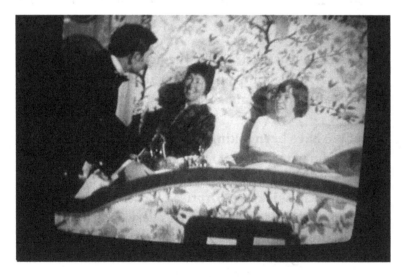

**"GOOD MORNING MY LADY –
BREAKFAST IS SERVED"**

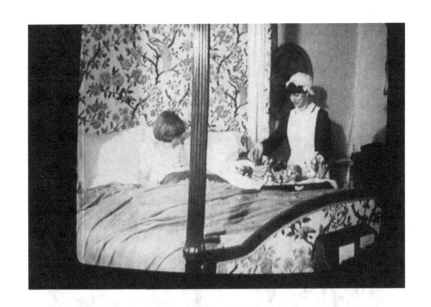

"MORE TEA MADAM?"

**A DREAM COMES TRUE
FOR ALISON**

PHOTO COURTESY OF THE EVENING HERALD NEWSPAPER – PLYMOUTH DEVON

I made the headlines in several
newspapers. The Evening Herald wrote:-

Alison the aristocrat

A light breakfast in stately style for 14-year-old
ALISON KERR as she awoke in a four poster
bed at Saltram House. Acting as maid and
butler are the cook and caretaker of the house,
Deirdre Davidson and Jack Swatton

Schoolgirl to
the manor born

SCHOOLGIRL Alison Kerr never believed bed and
breakfast could be so good. But the stately homes of
England can be relied on to do things in style.

When she spent last night at Saltram House it was in a 1760
four-poster bed with a full breakfast served on priceless
silver.

For disabled Alison, from Woodland Way, Torpoint, it was
a dream come true.

S h e w o k e u p t o d a y surrounded by aristocratic
elegance in the bedroom kept ready for occasional visits by
Lord and Lady Morley.

The first time she visited Saltram with the Dame Hannah
Roger's School at Ivybridge, she fell in love with it. And
when Ivybridge Round Table heard her biggest wish was to
stay there they played fairy g o d m o t h e r and approached
the National Trust.

After that it wasn't long before she was being escorted up the wide staircase for a candle-lit supper with the administrator and his wife, Martin and Mary Knebel.

Mugs

While her mother Maureen Kerr slept in the adjacent dressing room, Alison retired to Lord Morley's bedroom complete with Chippendale 1760 four-poster, wardrobe and early 18th century Chinese mugs.

"I was looking at the room for about two hours before I finally fell asleep," said Alison, 14, as she received guests at her bedside this morning with a smile.

The breakfast, like the bedroom, was five star. Cereal with cream, a grill, toast and home-made marmalade followed by coffee were all served off the 18th century family silver by Saltram cook Deirdre Davidson doubling as the housemaid.

Meanwhile, caretaker Jack Swatton was acting the part of butler in the one remaining set of family livery.

"I wasn't sure if I'd ever actually stay here but when they said I could I was really happy," beamed Alison.

On her bed was a bunch of carnations from one admirer and a telegram from another: "Sleep well princess, sweet dreams from Prince Charming."

Delighted

"I think this is a good life. But if I could live here I'd like to have done it in the old days rather than now because of the dresses," said Alison.

Her mother was delighted with the generosity of the Saltram House staff.

"I think its an enormous privilege to stay and sleep in a stately home. The National Trust have been superb – I don't think Alison will ever be the same again."

Alison, of Woodland Way, Torpoint was receiving visitors from her big comfy four poster until mid morning. Then she got up, dressed and was conducted down the wide staircase past the Stubbs and portrait of Sir Joshua Reynolds like a lady to the manor born .....

ALISON AND MUM AT SALTRAM HOUSE

The Ivybridge Gazette wrote:-

To the manor born

ALISON KERR, a 14-year-old Ivybridge schoolgirl, played the part of a lady this week as if she was born to it when she stayed one night in a stately home.

This for Alison was a dream come true: to sleep in a 1760 four-poster bed at Saltram House. When she woke up surrounded by Chippendale furniture and expensive antiques she had to pinch herself to make sure it was not a dream.

From the moment Alison arrived at the house on Monday evening she was treated like a lady.

Ivybridge Round Table was the driving force behind the event after Alison wrote to Tim Hardwick and his Tim'll Fix It scheme to ask if a night in Saltram was possible. After that it was over to the National Trust to make the final arrangements.

On Monday Alison was joined by her mother and father and Mike Abbott, Tim Hardwick and Mike Tudor from the Round Table while she had a candlelit meal.

Then the lady-for-a-night retired to her four-poster bed in Lord Morley's room, with her mother placed next door in the dressing room.

Alison woke up in the morning to be greeted by a butler and maid ready to serve her breakfast from priceless silver. Feeling quite at home, she tucked into cereal, a grill, marmalade and toast and coffee and was then ready to meet television film crews and flashing lights of numerous photographers.

Tim Hardwick told the Gazette: "It was worth it to us just to see her face, she was absolutely delighted and took it all in her stride. She beamed at the photographers and enjoyed every minute in the house."

When Alison, who is disabled, returns to Dame Hannah Rogers School on Monday she will have plenty to tell her friends.

Yes, I certainly did have plenty to tell my friends when I returned to school. Everyone was saying, "Oh Alison, I saw you on the television, I saw you in the newspapers and I heard you on the radio."

I was also asked to give a talk in assembly about my very very enjoyable stay at Saltram House. Everybody was extremely envious!

To remember my "Saltram" experience,
I compiled yet another scrapbook, in
which I put all my newspaper cuttings
and photographs.

Martin and Mary Knebel sent me
this letter:-

The National Trust for Places of Historic Interest or Natural Beauty
Saltram House, Plympton, Plymouth, PL7 3UH
Telephone: Plymouth (0752) 336546

Administrator: MARTIN KNEBEL

8th November 1980

Dear Alison,

Thank you for your letter and for coming to Saltram in
the first place. It really was very nice for us to enjoy the time
with you and your family and to share in all the excitement.

I agree the television was very good and we were able
to see it on both channels. It never ceases to surprise me how
imaginatively these professionals can build up the
programmes.

Jack and Deirdre did very well I thought. Jack has now
been promoted to look after a House in Staffordshire called
Shugbrook. Deirdre fortunately will continue as Cook.

Ray Hillgrove who had dinner with us has produced
some very good slides and I will see you get a set.

Please do call and see us again, perhaps when we open
again in April as the furniture is now under dust sheets and
much winter work is being undertaken.

With our Love and Best Wishes,

Martin & Mary Knebel

I did return to Saltram on one or two occasions, to have a look at my (Lord Morley's) bed again! Martin and Mary also invited Mum, Dad and I to the 1980 Christmas Carol concert which took place in The Saloon at Saltram – that was a very enjoyable occasion.

**ALISON SITTING AMONGST THE DAFFODILLS
IN THE GROUNDS OF ANTONY HOUSE –
ANOTHER NATIONAL TRUST PROPERTY
SITUATED NOT FAR FROM TORPOINT CORNWALL**

From October 1980 to July 1982, I participated in the Duke of Edinburgh's Award Scheme gaining both my Bronze and Silver Award.

Participating in such a scheme was hard work, but at the same time very very enjoyable. I also gained a great sense of achievement. Some reports in my Duke of Edinburgh's Award Record Book read:-

**BRONZE AWARD – FORM OF SERVICE
POLICE
DATE STARTED: 13-10-80
DATE COMPLETED: 8-12-80**

Alison attended all the lectures. Enjoyed her visit to Police Headquarters at Plympton and showed interest throughout the course. Gained an excellent assessment of 70%.

**D Reed
Police Constable No. 104**

BRONZE AWARD – SKILLS
NATURAL HISTORY – WILD FLOWERS
DATE STARTED: 1-10-80
DATE COMPLETED: 30-7-81

Alison has taken a great interest in identifying and classifying wild flowers. She has learnt a great deal about the flowering plant and flowering families and has kept an accurate record of the expeditions and observations made over the seasons.

G Davies
Biology Teacher

SILVER AWARD
FORM OF SERVICE
POLICE
DATE STARTED: JANUARY 1982
DATE COMPLETED: MARCH 1982

A good written account of the visit to the Communications Dept. and Charge Rooms at Crownhill. Also to Plympton Magistrates Court in full session. Well done. 65%.

D Reed
Police Constable 104

SILVER AWARD
SKILLS – NATURE
DATE STARTED: 20/10/81
DATE COMPLETED: 22/6/82

Alison has taken a great interest in following the lives of various birds through the changing season. She has conscientiously kept up her nature diary and made it a complete record of all her activities over the period of study.

She has been studying a pair of swans over the last three months and has made accurate observations on their habits as they nested and raised their cygnets. Altogether a worthwhile piece of work.

G Davies
Teacher

For the Physical Recreation part of my Duke of Edinburgh's Silver Award, I decided to participate in the sport of canoeing. Julia joined me for this and we had great fun together.

Because Julia and I were absolute beginners we learnt to canoe in the swimming pool at HMS Fisguard, in Torpoint, before progressing several weeks later, to Plymouth Sound.

Julia and I, and the rest of our team, became very adventurous, because not only did we all canoe from Plymouth Hoe out to the Break-Water, but also to the Tamar Bridges – starting, again from Plymouth Hoe.

**ALISON LOOKING AND FEELING
EXTREMELY NERVOUS AFTER HER FIRST
CAPSIZE!!!**

I haven't got any idea of the
distance between Plymouth Hoe and the
Tamar Bridges, but when you are only
canoeing at a snail's pace of about one
knot per hour, the distance seems
absolutely endless. I canoed under the
Tamar Bridges nursing several blisters,
as well as feeling extremely shattered!

**ALISON WITH TONY DUNCAN
AT SHEPTON MALLET IN DEVON –
WHERE PRINCE PHILIP
THE DUKE OF EDINBURGH
WAS PRESENT**

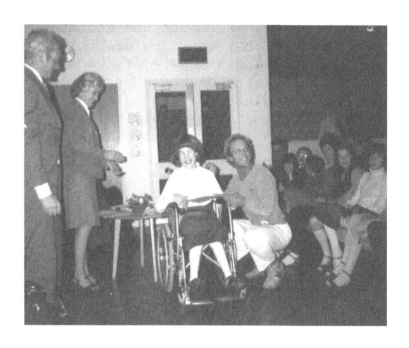

**ALISON RECEIVING HER SILVER
DUKE OF EDINBURGH'S AWARD
FROM BRIAN JACKS**

Sitting in my canoe under the Tamar Bridges, certainly was not the first time I nursed blisters.

For three consecutive years, (1980–1982) I participated in the Ten Tors Special Event across Dartmoor.

In order to qualify, I had to prove that I could independently propel my wheelchair on roads for a distance of 6½ miles, regardless of any incline whether it be up or down.

Obviously I had to do a lot of training beforehand which involved a huge amount of determination, endurance and, despite wearing padded gloves, several blisters – but it was all worthwhile in the end, especially when I received a Bronze, Silver and Gold medal for all my effort.

Nicole Summers carries camping equipment up the gang plank of the mini bus for the Ten Tors walk. Also taking part are, from left, Alison Kerr, Charles Penno and Grant Harrison, from Dame Hannah Rogers School, Ivybridge.

ALISON AND A FEW OF HER SCHOOL FRIENDS ABOUT TO TACKLE DARTMOOR!!

A few extracts from my 1982 diary read:-

WEDNESDAY 12TH MAY 1982

This afternoon I went on my final Ten Tors practice, because I am doing the actual 'push' on Saturday. I'm a bit apprehensive about it now, I don't know whether to do it now or not – I suppose I've got to, and I'm going to!

FRIDAY 14TH MAY 1982

This afternoon Mary Bounds, Tony Duncan, Greta Johns, David Watson, Jack Gates, Charles Penno, Grant Harrison, Nicole Summers and myself, all set off towards Okehampton to take part in the Ten Tors Expedition of 1982.

When we arrived at Okehampton Army Camp everyone was rushing about putting their tents up. The weather was quite nice; the sun was shining, but the wind was a bit fresh.

In the evening after our briefing on the rules of the Ten Tors Special Event, we met our Junior Leaders. My man is called Graham, and he seems very nice.

At about 9.15 pm, we all went to bed because we've got to get up at 4.30 am, in order to begin our walk (in my case, 'push') at 7.30 am tomorrow!!

SATURDAY 15TH MAY 1982

"Good morning Campers, it is 4.30 am and it is time to get up!" That was the sentence which was blastered over the campsite at such an early hour of the morning, along with the tune of "Onward Christian Soldiers," etc., etc!! I certainly did not feel like going 'onward' at that time of the morning, I just wanted to roll over in my nice cosy sleeping bag and go back to sleep! That wasn't to be the case. I thought to myself, "I've been waiting for today for a long time, so I'm absolutely determined to make a go of it now!"

To reach the starting point by 7.30 am, the Army blokes very kindly escorted us in their trucks, and I can assure you that that was quite an adventure in itself! I have never been so thrown about in all my life, and they certainly know how to use the brakes!! I was extremely relieved to get out!!

Despite being so apprehensive, I thoroughly enjoyed the walk – you know what I mean! I don't know who was more tired though, myself or Graham! There were several steep hills which I had to tackle; one which went on for half a mile and that took me an hour and twenty five minutes to complete. I certainly made good time going down the hills though, especially if the wind was pointing in the right direction! I would just let my wheelchair free-wheel down the hill and hope for the best! Meanwhile though, poor old Graham was running for his life desperately trying to keep up with me! It was great fun!

I completed the course at 1.45 pm this afternoon, and needless to say, despite almost falling asleep sitting up, I was feeling really chuffed with myself; as I achieved what I've always wanted, a Gold Medal!!

I must point out that to receive my Ten Tors certificates and medals, I had to improve on my finishing time each year.

My brother Pete took part in the Ten Tors main event twice, and we met each other at the finishing point – what an excellent feeling that was for both of us!

Pete was required to walk 35 miles for his Bronze medal, and 45 miles for his Silver medal – spending the night camping on Dartmoor as well.

ALISON FEELING VERY TIRED –
BUT EXTREMELY PLEASED WITH HERSELF

ALISON AND LARRY
ENJOYING A DRINK IN CHELTENHAM

CHAPTER THREE

TWO YEARS IN THE COTSWOLDS

NATIONAL STAR CENTRE FOR DISABLED YOUTH
ULLLENWOOD MANOR
CHELTENHAM
GLOUCESTERSHIRE
GL53 9QU

They say that all good things have
to come to an end, and sadly in July
1982, my days at Dame Hannah's did just
that.

I really enjoyed my time at Dame
Hannah Rogers School and have a lot of
very happy memories.

A member of staff gave me a notelet
which read:-

23.7.'82

Dear Alison,

All my good wishes go with you for happiness in
all you do. I'm sure you will prove to be one of Dame
Hannah's shining stars.

Fond love from

Audin (Kenyon)

"I was extremely touched to receive
such a kind note - thank you very very
much Audin."

In September 1982, a new chapter in
my life was opened. I became a student
at the National Star Centre, a
specialised college of Further
Education for Disabled Youth, in
Cheltenham.

Mum, Dad and Julia drove me to
Cheltenham initially - then every other
journey to and from college, I made
independently - the majority by train.

All new students had to arrive two
days prior to the older students
returning to college, in order to
familiarise themselves with their new
surroundings.

I can remember very clearly, looking
out the window of the Manor House,
thinking to myself, "I am here for the
next two years - I wonder what they have
in store for me?"

**A VIEW OF THE COLLEGE LAKE
FROM THE MANOR HOUSE**

A few minutes later one of the other new students came over to me and said, "My name is Lawrence, but I prefer to be known as Larry."

Following Larry's introduction, as time passed by, we spent more and more time together, and fellow students kept saying to Larry, "Why don't you ask her out?" Larry did, but it wasn't love at first sight!

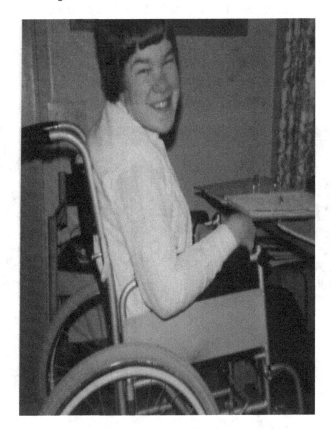

**ALISON STUDYING IN HER ROOM
AT COLLEGE**

Larry would, on the odd occasion, get fed up with me because I would literally spend hours (weekends included) in my room studying. I said to Larry, "All this studying will pay off in the end."

Yes, Larry was right, I did do a lot
of studying, but I thought that was the
main reason for coming to college in the
first place – to gain further
qualifications. I left Dame Hannah's
with just three academic qualifications
which didn't really satisfy me. I knew
I could do better if I put my mind to
it.

Talking of Dame Hannah's, John
Logue, the Medical Officer at college,
was very friendly with Joanne Slade, and
once I told John that I knew Joanne from
my days at Dame Hannah's, we all became
very close, and as a result, spent quite
a bit of time together.

JOHN WITH HIS THREE DOGS

JOANNE WITH HER PARENTS
AT THEIR FAMILY HOME IN WEYMOUTH DORSET

"JOANNE WAS ABOUT TO COMPLETE HER TIME AT
DAME HANNAH ROGERS SCHOOL IN 1976 -
WHEN I BECAME A PUPIL"

During my two years as a student at the National Star Centre I was determined to make the most of all the facilities on offer.

I thoroughly enjoyed having driving lessons in a mini with Roger, the College Driving Instructor, as that gave me a great sense of independence. When the day of my test arrived though, it was a totally different matter - I was extremely nervous! Roger left me sitting in the mini outside the Cheltenham Test Centre, and when I saw the Examiner approaching, I thought to myself, "Oh my god, he looks really serious!"

On my return to the Test Centre I knew what the Examiner's final sentence was going to be, "I am sorry to have to tell you Miss Kerr, but you have failed your driving test on this occasion."

The drive back to college was not a happy one, but I was not going to give up learning to drive.

**ALISON AFTER A DRIVING LESSON
WITH ROGER**

One of Roger's many successful
students was Larry McGovern. Larry
passed his driving test second time
round. When Larry returned to college
and told me of his success, I was really
happy for him.

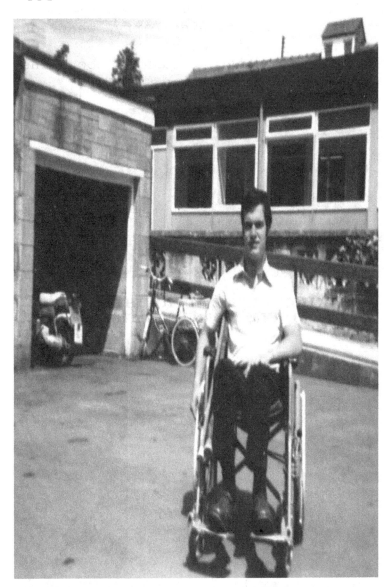

LARRY McGOVERN

I may have not been successful with
my first driving test, but I was always
looking for new challenges to set
myself.

Having completed both the Bronze and
Silver Duke of Edinburgh's Award, I was
delighted when I was given the
opportunity to work for the Gold Award.

For the weekend of 19th November to
20th November 1983, myself, and several
other people, including Larry, went on a
preliminary training weekend to
Stratford-Upon-Avon, learning about the
Youth Hostel Association.

**ALISON OUTSIDE THE YOUTH HOSTEL
IN STRATFORD-UPON-AVON**

**LARRY ALISON AND LYNN
OUTSIDE SHAKESPEARE'S BIRTHPLACE –
STRATFORD-UPON-AVON**

Our weekend in Stratford-Upon-Avon proved to be very educational and enjoyable.

The actual Exploration for my Gold Duke of Edinburgh's Award took place in Pembrokeshire, Wales, from 14th April to 19th April 1984, where an exploration of the coast and local crafts was completed.

LARRY AND ALISON BEING TOLD ALL ABOUT THE WORKING OF A MILL

STUDIOUS LARRY!

LYNN AND ALISON

LYNN AND ALISON ADMIRING THE VIEW

On completion of my few days away in Pembrokeshire, the following was written in my Duke of Edinburgh's Award Record Book:-

Alison's participation on this exploration was 100%. Her involvement was an active endeavour to battle on at all costs. She completed everything that was asked of her.

Her account was very neat and accurate and colourful. Very informative and she certainly gained a lot of knowledge of Pembrokeshire during training and the actual Exploration.

Chris Crosskey
D of E Leader

Alison was eager to have a go at mapping and compass work – she proved very quick at picking things up, even though she was hindered by her wheelchair when it came to compass work; the metal in the chair affected the compass. She successfully completed a short compass course.

She enjoyed the short jaunts into the countryside although the hills often proved too much for her. She also spent one night under canvas; a feat she has every right to be proud of.

David Hughes
7th Chelt. C/Kings Ventures

It was only one month after returning from Wales that I was taken off the college campus again, but it was certainly not through choice! An ambulance was called to take me to Cheltenham General Hospital where I underwent an operation to have my appendix removed later that night.

I received lots of visitors during my time in hospital – Mum, Dad and Larry, to name just a few. I even spent my 18th birthday in hospital which wasn't very good timing on my part!

Being ill is a huge inconvenience to me! By the end of May 1984, I was back in the saddle literally, completing the Physical Recreation section of my Gold Duke of Edinburgh's Award.

ALISON BACK IN THE SADDLE!

I attended riding lessons at Camp
Riding Centre, near Stroud, between
March 1983 and May 1984. The following
remarks were also written in my Record
Book:-

Alison has developed a quite impressive ability to
rise at the trot and to handle the reins, and shows
increased confidence.

She is never just a "passenger" and likes to control
the pony herself, with a little support. Good work.

Alison has been such a pleasant and valuable
member of the "team" and has managed "smiling
riding" even when tired! Her written account of all
equine activities is superb, so good in fact that her book
has been passed around all Red Cross helpers, from
Riding Club to Branch H.Q.

A great promotional piece of work!

Thank you Alison! Well done!

S M Barron

Driving a mini and riding on
horseback were not the only methods of
transport which I had control of while I
was a student in Cheltenham. There was
a third - a motor glider!!!

In June 1984, fellow students and
staff and myself, were invited as guests
of the RAF to a base in Wiltshire, near
Chippenham, to experience motor gliding.
Such an invitation could not be refused,
so off we all went feeling very excited.

Before I was allowed to reach for
the sky, the pilot, Peter, asked me to
sign a form for insurance purposes -

just in case we decided to glide off to
heaven and never appear on earth again!!

"ARE YOU SITTING COMFORTABLY ALISON?"

ALISON EAGER TO TAKE OFF!!!

"HERE WE GO" SAYS ALISON!!!

It wasn't long before Peter was given the all clear for take off and we were speeding down the runway. All of a sudden we were lifted off the ground and gaining height at a rapid rate of knots! At that moment I lost my stomach, but couldn't go back to find it!!

When we had reached 1,700 feet and were further away from the runway, Peter said, "I'm going to switch the engine off now, and we are just going to glide through the air."

Gliding, I thought was absolutely fantastic. It is so peaceful and you are away from the hustle and bustle of everyday life. You are also obviously

77

seeing the world from a totally different angle, which is quite an experience in itself.

I enjoyed the first flight so much that I asked Peter if I could take to the sky for a second time!

During our second flight Peter asked, "Would you like to fly the plane?" I couldn't believe my ears!! I thought to myself, "Does he really mean that? I'll probably crash the thing and that will be the end for both of us!" I did have a go at flying the plane myself, and found it very enjoyable.

I can't say that I enjoyed the landing part of the flight. We came down with such a thump, which I must admit, did frighten me. The second landing wasn't as bad as the first though, because I knew what was ahead of me!!

ALISON SAFELY BACK ON THE GROUND!!!

Whilst on the subject of flying, during my couple of years as a student at the National Star Centre, and on two separate occasions, very important people visited the college - their transport was the Queen's Flight. Those very important people were Her Royal Highness, the Duchess of Kent, and Diana, the Princess of Wales.

**THE QUEEN'S FLIGHT HELICOPTER
IN THE COLLEGE GROUNDS**

**ALLEN FIELD (COLLEGE PRINCIPAL)
HRH THE DUCHESS OF KENT
HELEN DUNNIPACE (COLLEGE LECTURER)
STUDENTS – CHARMAINE ALISON ROB AND MORRIS**

DIANA PRINCESS OF WALES

I felt extremely honoured to have the opportunity to meet such special ladies. Diana said "Hello" to me, which may not seem much, but I shall remember her saying just that one word to me, for the rest of my life.

Ever since I have lived in England I have been a big fan of the Royal Family.

To conclude "Two Years in the
Cotswolds," I would like to share my
college report with you:-

NATIONAL STAR CENTRE FOR DISABLED YOUTH
A SPECIALISED COLLEGE OF FURTHER EDUCATION

ULLENWOOD MANOR – CHELTENHAM – GLOUCESTERSHIRE – GL53 9QU
TELEPHONE (0242) 27631 – APPEALS: (0242) 24478

Patron: H.R.H The Duchess of Kent – President: Her Grace The Duchess of Beaufort – Principal: Allen Field, LCP, MRIPHH, F Coll P.

COURSE: City and Guilds 691 – Foundation Certificate   (Commercial Studies)

STUDENT: ALISON KERR

PERSONAL TUTOR: Mr Gresswell   SUMMER TERM 1984

STUDY AREAS:

Industrial, Social and Environmental Studies:

The Social and Physical Environment – Alison is a
very quiet girl in lessons. She works extremely hard
in her own time to type up her notes and to produce
some excellent work. She also takes every
opportunity to borrow material offered and to work
on it – again in her own time. She deserves success.

The Working Environment – Alison has spent a lot of
time and effort in producing some excellent
coursework. Hopefully her medical problems will
not adversely affect her performance in the
examinations, since this would be a great shame,
considering all the work she has put in during the rest
of the course.

Office Skills and Practices:

Typewriting – Alison produces neat, accurate, well
displayed work. Her conscientious attitude is shown
clearly in everything she produces. She will be taking

the Pitman's Elementary Examination in July and could be a very useful typist, given a more intensive course.

Clerical Skills – Alison works slowly but perseveres at everything she does. Her work is accurate and neat and she copes with most clerical activities.

Commercial Technology, Theory and Science:

Alison has been one of the most determined and hardworking members of the group and she is to be commended on the way in which she has persevered to overcome her debilitating medical problems. She always takes great care with her work and it has been of a very good quality, with particular care taken over neatness and display.

Communication Studies:

Literacy – Alison is a good, neat worker. Careful and painstaking, gaining her C & G Level 1 examination in December 1983. She has the tenacity of purpose as well as the potential to carry on her language work to higher public examination levels. An exemplary student.

Numeracy – Alison has worked very hard throughout the course; although she has found the work difficult she has made steady progress. She works neatly and carefully. She will be taking the C & G Level 1 exam before she leaves.

Guidance:

Although Alison is not very forthcoming in discussion groups, she has gradually gained in confidence and become more willing to put forward her point of view.

Optional Activities:

Occupational Therapy – Alison has tackled a wide range of light craft work and has gained a lot from doing so. Her work is always of a good standard.

Personal Tutor:

Alison has made full use of all the activities here, for both studying and developing life skills. This is reflected in her work record and I wish her well for the future.

Summary:

Alison has done well. She hopes to continue her education at the Mid-Cornwall Technical College from a base at the Kerensa hostel.

We wish Alison well for the future and hope she will keep in touch with us through the Old Students' Association.

Signed: *Allen Field*

• •

A. Field – Principal

KERENSA HOSTEL

CHAPTER FOUR

NO TEA FOR ALISON

ALISON AT KERENSA

KERENSA HOSTEL
TRURO ROAD
ST AUSTELL
CORNWALL

On 29th July 1984 I was once again known as the new girl! I became a resident at Kerensa.

Briefly, Kerensa catered for people living in Cornwall who were faced with all kinds of disabilities, mainly as a result of a road traffic accident.

Strangely enough, my first day at Kerensa followed the same pattern as my first day at the National Star Centre in Cheltenham. I found myself looking out of a window in the hostel admiring the view of St. Austell Town Centre, and wondering what life at Kerensa was going to be like.

Later that day, I was introduced by a member of staff called Jenny, to another member of staff, whose name escapes me. Jenny's words were, "This is Alison, who is a new admission today."

To be totally honest, Jenny's words upset me. I thought, "Why is she using the word "admission" because I am not in hospital?!"

Not long after my so called admission to Kerensa I phoned home to find out whether my examination results had arrived. Dad answered the phone, and in a teasing mood he said, "You've failed!" I then eagerly asked Dad to read my exam results to me, which were as follows:-

City & Guilds London Institute –	
Industrial Social & Environmental Studies	*Pass/Distinction*
City & Guilds London Institute –	
Office Skills & Practice	*Distinction/Distinction*
City & Guilds London Institute –	
Commercial Technology, Theory & Science	*Credit/Distinction*
City & Guilds London Institute –	
Communication Studies	*Credit/Credit*
City & Guilds London Institute –	
Numeracy Level One	*Pass*
City & Guilds London Institute –	
Communication Skills Level One	*Pass/Credit*
English Speaking Board –	
Vocational Grade One	*Credit*
English Speaking Board –	
Certificate in Spoken English for Higher Education	*Credit*
Pitmans –	
Typewriting Elementary	*Pass*

After speaking to Dad I was feeling **very very** pleased with myself. All my studying had paid off – and my health problems (gynaecological) thankfully did not affect my performance in the examinations.

Still eager to continue with my studies, on 4th September 1984, I enrolled as a full-time student at Mid Cornwall College of Further Education – in St. Austell. The course which I chose to study, for approximately ten months, was the Business Education Council General Diploma Award in Business Studies.

Enrolling as a student at Mid Cornwall College was quite an achievement in itself, because for the very first time in my life I was

experiencing mainstream education. I
was the only student out of 600,
confined to a wheelchair. I was also
the only young lady in a class of 8
young men!

To increase my independence, on 2nd
October 1984 I bought myself a Power
Plus electric wheelchair, which meant
that I was now able to drive myself
from Kerensa to college and vice-versa,
as well as around St. Austell as a
whole.

**ALISON SITTING IN THE GROUNDS OF
MID CORNWALL COLLEGE OF FURTHER EDUCATION
ST AUSTELL CORNWALL**

Just when I thought life was being
pretty good to me, as I had settled in
well at Kerensa, bought myself an
electric wheelchair and was making good
progress with my course at college, I
experienced a huge shock.

The day was Monday 9th October 1984. I was feeling pleased and happy with myself because my Typing tutor, Mary Quantrell had given me top marks for my first typing exercise.

Mary wrote the following:-

- 8 OCT 1984

<u>Alison</u>

This is absolutely first-class work. <u>Very</u> well done!

Will you please now work your way through the list of work I gave you – let me have each folder for marking as you complete it.

<u>As fast as you can please.</u> I want to put you onto practice exam papers as soon as possible. <u>You</u> are good!!

Incidentally, Mary chose to be my unofficial personal typing tutor. Officially she was employed to tutor students who were studying to become medical secretaries.

Now – I won't keep you in suspense anymore with regard to my huge shock. I must warn you though that it was by no means pleasant and I certainly **would not** like to repeat the experience ever.

The time was around five o'clock. All the hostel residents, including myself, had gathered in the dining room for our evening meal. Anne, one of the hostel cooks had just placed a pot full of tea in the middle of the table which I was sharing with two other residents called Marlene and Sylvia.

While we were all waiting for the hostel care staff to come into the dining room, because both hostel residents and staff shared the same dining room, I decided as usual, to pour myself a cup of tea.

Unfortunately I didn't get round to drinking that cup of tea. I had just picked the teapot up when suddenly, to my absolute horror, my hand suffered a muscle spasm or an involuntary tremor, and the teapot full of boiling hot tea and tea bags fell into my lap.

The pain I suffered that evening was excruciating – I screamed out in absolute agony.

My memories of the events that followed next are very patchy. I do remember though, a member of the hostel staff saying, while I was having my clothes cut off, that an ambulance had been called to take me to hospital, and that Tammy was going to be in the ambulance with me.

Treliske Hospital in Truro was to be my home for the next fortnight, and due to the severity of my burns, anybody who came into contact with me had to wear white gowns, to prevent the spread of infection.

On my return to Kerensa, I was told that a District Nurse would be visiting me daily to change my dressings. I must say that I was extremely grateful to the District Nurse for changing my dressings, but I was certainly far from grateful when I was informed by the hostel staff that I would be having a cold bath every morning. I would dread the thought of having to get out of bed! Apparently they were instructed

by the District Nurse to give me a cold
bath, as it was part of the healing
process for my burns. After literally
pleading with the hostel staff not to
give me any more cold baths, I was told
that I was being given the wrong
treatment! "Thank god for that," I
thought!

Despite my unfortunate setback, I
was determined to carry on with my
studies. I also accepted that I had a
lot of study time to make up. In order
to achieve this, I don't mind admitting
that I did burn the candle at both ends
on several occasions!!

I thoroughly enjoyed being a student
at Mid Cornwall College of Further
Education - as I made lots of friends -
both students and staff, and was
extremely grateful to be given the
opportunity to continue with my
education in order to achieve a very
worthwhile qualification.

**ALISON ATTENDING
ONE OF HER MANY LECTURES**

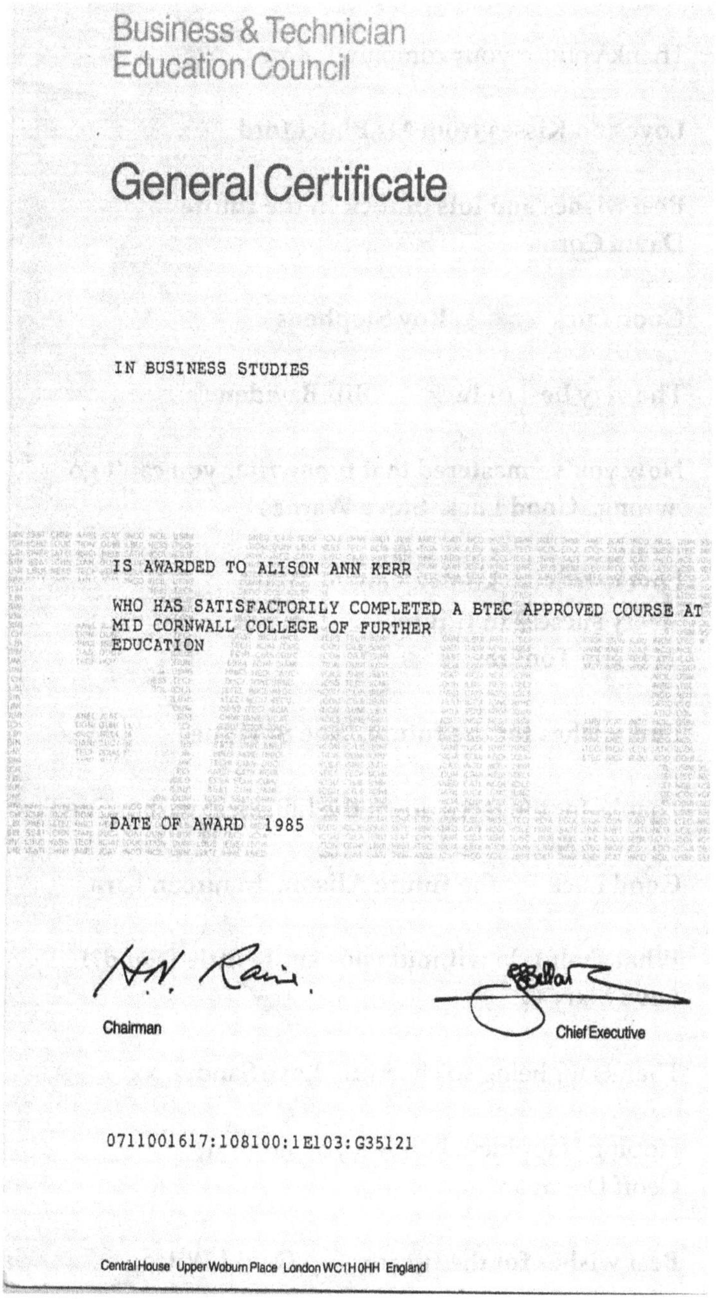

Business & Technician
Education Council

General Certificate

IN BUSINESS STUDIES

IS AWARDED TO ALISON ANN KERR

WHO HAS SATISFACTORILY COMPLETED A BTEC APPROVED COURSE AT
MID CORNWALL COLLEGE OF FURTHER
EDUCATION

DATE OF AWARD 1985

H.N. Rane.

Chairman

Bullar

Chief Executive

0711001617:108100:1E103:G35121

Central House Upper Woburn Place London WC1H 0HH England

    I received a lovely card to mark my
departure - signed by various members
of staff.

    Surrounded by *With Best Wishes* the
following messages were written inside
my card:-

To Alison

Thank you for your company! Kate

Love and Kisses from Mr Blatchford   x

**Best wishes and lots of luck in the future
David Corns**

Good Luck   Roy Stephens

The very best of luck   Bill Bawden

**Now you've mastered that typewriter you can't go
 wrong. Good Luck Steve Warnes**

**Lovely to have known you,
 every success in future.
 Nanette Tonkin**

Best wishes for the future. Sue Spragne

Thanks for the races down the hill. Best wishes Sue Fox

Good Luck for the future Alison. Maureen Larn

**What shall I do without your smile little friend?
Love Mary Q**

Thanks for being so cheerful. Love Sandra xx

Hoping Happiness Follows you around.
Geoff Donovan

Best wishes for the future.   David Wilson

I shall miss your smiling face outside my office –
lots of luck in the future. Penny x

Best wishes and lots of luck Di Goom

With all good wishes Alison. Owen and Anne Moon

**A 'STUDY SATISFIED' ALISON –
WITH BRIAN**

Eighteen months later my burns had
unfortunately not healed properly - and
were continuing to give me pain. I was
therefore referred to a Plastic Surgeon
and subsequently admitted to Derriford
Hospital in Plymouth for an operation.
I was very nervous at the thought of
having yet another operation, but also
looking forward to being free of pain
after such a long period of time.

CHAPTER
FIVE

A
JUMBULANCE
HOLIDAY IN
AUSTRIA

ALISON AND BOB
ARRIVING IN ST WOLFGANG – AUSTRIA

"AUSTRIA HERE I COME!!!"

I believe that if you work hard, you should reward yourself by playing hard too!! That is exactly what I did after completing my course at Mid Cornwall College of Further Education. From 4th to 13th October 1985, I experienced, 'A Jumbulance Holiday in Austria' – it was great fun, to say the least!!!

First of all, let me put you completely in the picture with regard to Jumbulance travel, courtesy of the Across Trust – in 1985:-

The ACROSS Trust is a Registered Charity formed in 1972 to build and operate a jumbo-ambulance called a Jumbulance, purpose built to travel over long distances groups of severely sick and handicapped people of all ages on tours, holidays and pilgrimages ACROSS Europe. There is now a fleet of ten Jumbulances; five standard Jumbulances costing £85,000 each, capacity 24 persons; three Alligator (double) Jumbulances costing £176,000 each, capacity 44 persons; and two mini-Jumbulances costing £33,000 each, capacity 24. Each standard and alligator Jumbulance averages 100,000 miles per year. By December 1984 over 1,280 groups travelled ACROSS totalling over 30,000 passengers. ACROSS, a non-denominational organisation, makes the seemingly impossible, possible for the severely handicapped and very sick.

Each Jumbulance (excluding mini-Jumbulances) is fitted with tubular aluminium beds adjustable for back and knee posture, reclining seats, a toilet, hydraulic lifting platform, a kitchen with refrigerator, hot and cold water, hot and cold meals and beverages, as on an aircraft, oxygen, ripple mattress, suction unit, respiratory equipment and standard medical supplies. Blankets, pillows and bed linen are provided on the Jumbulance. There are a number of elevating trolley-beds and collapsible wheelchairs available. Arrangements can be made, on request, (before travelling), for handicapped passengers requiring these on holiday.

Before going on holiday, whether it is to a destination abroad or close to home – there are still vital preparations which have to be adhered to in order for the holiday to run as smoothly as possible.

It was Jane and Sheila who did most of the preparations for our holiday to St. Wolfgang in Austria. I would like to take this opportunity to thank them both, as they worked extremely hard organising several fundraising events in an attempt to lower the cost of our fares. Their biggest hurdle was finding enough people who could not only volunteer their help, but also afford to pay their own fare.

MEVAGISSEY ACROSS HOLIDAY GROUP

The Jays Nest,
Trevarth,
Mevagissey,
Tele. 842680

Dear Alison,

We are so pleased that you have shown interest in our holiday to St. Wolfgang, Austria, 4th – 13th Oct. 85, fare approx. £290.

We are delighted to have some many enquiries about the holiday, but this makes our job most difficult in compiling our passenger list. The formation of an ACROSS group is a complex task with many factors to be considered.

Our head office gives priority

(a) to those with terminal illness.

(b) those confined to bed, wheelchair and four walls.

(c) those with progressive disease or condition which makes other means of transport impossible, or unsuitable, after which those with less complicated handicaps are considered.

Six months prior to departure date (ie 4th April) we must submit our final list to head office for their approval. If your name is on this list we will notify you and in due course you will be sent forms for you and your doctor to complete, and when these have been processed we will require a deposit of £30.

Insurance cover for the holiday is included in the fare. Cover comes into effect when the fare is paid in full. Balance payment of the holiday is required one month before departure date. Payment by instalments can be arranged.

Thank you for your interest.

Yours sincerely,

Jane Barron
Hon. Sec.

Sheila Daniel
Chairman.

Registered as a Charity in accordance with the War Charities Act 1940, National Assistance Act 1948, Charities Act 19
Charity Roll No. 265540

ACROSS

THE ACROSS TRUST,

CROWN HOUSE, MORDEN, SURREY, SM4 5EW, ENGLAND TEL: 01-540 3897

PASSENGER LIST

GROUP NO: 1446   TITLE: MEVAGISSEY/ST.WOLFGANG   JUMBULANCE MARK: 7

DATES: 4th - 13th October

DESTINATION Sports Hotel Wolfgangerhof

	NAME	ADDRESS
U	Christopher Baron	2 Beaconside, Foxhole, St. Austell, PL27 7UJ
U	William Chapman	33 Lower Bore St., Bodmin, Cornwall, PL31 2JU
U	Jack Ede	Weldun, Tregrehan Mills, St. Austell, PL25 3TG
U	Ian Hutchens	Great Brighter Farm, St. Kew Highway, Bodmin, PL30 3DR
U	Kevin Nichols	27 Coombe Park, Kingsand, Torpoint, PL10 1NY
U	Michael Webb	Kerenza, Truro Rd., St. Austell, PL25 0OO
U	Derek Williams	8 Lytton Place, St. Austell, PL25 4PE
U	Shirley Bennett	113 Phernyssick Rd., Boscoppa, St. Austell, PL25 3TZ
U	Effie Hunkin	32 Tregoney Hill, Mevagissey, PL26 6RE
U	Alison Kerr	Kerensa, Truro Road, St. Austell, PL25 0OO
U	Dorothy Lakeman	5 Battery Terrace, Mevagissey
U	Ethel Rickard	2 Trevanion Rd., Trewoon, St. Austell, PL25 5SY
U	Olive Snell	17 Ilex Avenue, Clevedon, Avon B521 6EE
U	Margaret Williams	Gwavas, Tregrehan, Par, Cornwall, PL24 2SJ

KEY		KEY TO PICK UPS	Assemble	Depart	Return
C	– Chaplain				
L	– Leader	1. Restormel Borough,	04.30	05.30	03.00 (14/
D	– Doctor	Council Offices,			
N	– Nurse	Car Park, Truro Rd.,			
Med.	– Medical Student	St. Austell, Cornwall.			
Ax.	– Aux. Nurse				
St.N.	– Student Nurse	2. "Leigh-Delamere"	08.00	08.15	24.00
Phy.	– Physiotherapist	Service Station,			(midnig
A	– Able	M4 Motorway.			
U	– Unable				
Ch	– Child				

TRUSTEES: J. CARVILL, M. K. DOWN, P. FLAVIN, R. V. GLITHERO, Y. NULTY

Registered as a Charity in accordance with the War Charities Act 1940, National Assistance Act 1948, Charities Act
Charity Roll No. 265540

ACROSS

THE ACROSS TRUST,

CROWN HOUSE, MORDEN, SURREY, SM4 5EW, ENGLAND TEL: 01-540 3897

PASSENGER LIST

GROUP NO: 1446	TITLE: MEVAGISSEY/St.WOLFGANG	JUMBULANCE MARK: 7

DATES: 4th - 13th October

DESTINATION Sports Hotel Wolfgangerhof

	NAME	ADDRESS
N	Peter Thompson	Flat 97, Kynance House, Royal Cornwall Hospital, Truro, TR13LJ
A	David Baron	2 Beaconside, Foxhole, St. Austell, Cornwall, PL26 7UJ
A	Stuart Cant	11 Brandon Road, Scunthorpe, S. Humbs, DN15 7HM
A	David Carr	Sunhaven, Rice Lane, Gorran Haven, St. Austell, PL26 6JD
A	Paul Gossan	The Haven, Cape, Canton St., Gorran Haven, St. Austell
A	Thomas Knowles	13 Parklands, Nanpean, St. Austell, Cornwall, PL26 7VR
A	James Philp	72 Polgrean, St. Blazey, Par, Cornwall, PL24 2LJ
A	Kenneth Williams	"Ewavas", Tregrehan, Par, Cornwall, PL24 2SJ
D	Rosalyn Mauchline	25 Henderson Court, East Calder, Lothian Region, EH53 ORQ
L	Jane Barron	The Jays Nest, Trevarth, Mevagissey, Cornwall
N	Elizabeth Pearce	11 Bloomfield Park Road, Timsbury, Bath, BA31 LN
N	Patricia Thompson	34 Eliot Road, St. Austell, Cornwall, PL25 4NN
A	Brenda Carr	Sunhaven, Rice Lane, Gorran Haven, St. Austell, PL26 6JD
A	Sheila Daniel	Polmenna, Portheast Way, Gorran Haven, St. Austell PL26 6JA
A	Georgina Dixon	Ravensbourne, Gonvena Hill, Wadebridge, PL27 6DM
A	Audrey Hoskins	Charnborough Farm, Holcombe, Bath, BA3 5EX
A	Eileen Pearce	Sunnyside, Penwarne Lane, Mevagissey, PL26 6PF
A	Louisa Powell	School Hill, Mevagissey, PL26 6TQ

KEY		KEY TO PICK UPS	Assemble	Depart	Return
C	– Chaplain				
L	– Leader				
D	– Doctor	1. Restormel Borough	04.30	05.30	03.00 (14,
N	– Nurse	Council Offices,			
Med.	– Medical Student	Car Park, Truro Rd.,			
Ax.	– Aux. Nurse	St. Austell, Cornwall.			
St.N.	– Student Nurse				
Phy.	– Physiotherapist	2. "Leigh-Delamere"	08.00	08.15	24.00
A	– Able	Service Station,			(midni
U	– Unable	M4 Motorway.			
Ch	– Child				

TRUSTEES: J. CARVILL, M. K. DON   FLAVIN, R. V. GLITHERO, Y. NULTY

'The Jays Nest'
Trevarth
Mevagissey
Cornwall

12th August 1985

Dear Alison,

As the time for our holiday draws closer,
we have to get down to the business side
of things, so please find enclosed the
bill. However, we can also start looking
forward to our holiday and really plan
for it. In this letter we hope you will
find some useful information.

You are allowed to take one suitcase,
which will travel in the hold of the
Jumbulance and you will not have access
to it until we reach Austria. Please
pack all medicines (including water
tablets if you take them), slippers and
wash things in a small hand luggage bag
which will stay with you on the bus.
Please make sure you also have your
passport and some English currency in
your hand luggage. The money is for use
on the ferry as they do not take Austrian
Schillings.

Money
For your stay in Austria the currency you
will need is Austrian Schillings which
can be bought at any bank. It does take
about ten days to come, so please place
your order in plenty of time.

Clothing
We suggest that you cater for all
weathers i.e. a sweater for chilly
evenings and a mac (with hood) for rain,
should we have any. Remember comfort is
the order of the day, wear clothes you
are happy in. If you can obtain a water-

proof wheelchair cover, it would be very beneficial to you. Don't forget your bathing costume and towel so that you can use the indoor heated swimming pool. During our stay we will be having a fancy dress party night, the theme of which will be 'TRAMPS AND TARTS' so if you have anything that may be suitable please bring it with you, however, dressing up is not compulsory.

Wallets
When we receive your travel wallet from H.Q. we will send it on to you. In it you will find your luggage labels and lots more useful information. Please read it all with care.

We cordially invite you to a 'GET TOGETHER BAR-B-Q', at Sheila's home 'POLMENA', Porth East Way, Gorran Haven, on Sunday September 15th at 4.00 p.m. R.S.V.P.

This is an opportunity to say 'Hello' to each other before we embark on our travels. We do hope you enjoy your holiday with us.

Yours sincerely

J Barron

J. Barron
Hon. Sec.

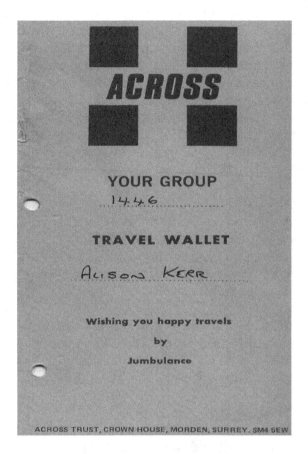

YOUR GROUP

1446

TRAVEL WALLET

Alison Kerr

Wishing you happy travels

by

Jumbulance

ACROSS TRUST, CROWN HOUSE, MORDEN, SURREY. SM4 5EW

YOUR HOLIDAY ADDRESS:-
SPORT HOTEL WOLFGANGERHOF
ST WOLFGANG AM SEE
SALZKAMMERGUT
AUSTRIA.

TELE. 010 436138/2237
OR   /2509

 For the duration of my holiday I
kept a diary - I'm very pleased I did,
as it was most definitely a holiday that
I shall never forget.

At long last the time has come for the
'holiday of a lifetime' to begin. I gave
Jane a ring in the evening of 3rd October,
just to make sure of the final
arrangements.

Later I finished packing my suitcase - or
suitcase and hand luggage bag, I should
say. Gave myself a bath and lay down on
my bed for a few hours until it was time
to go and meet the Jumbulance, which was
stationed at the Council Offices not far
from Kerensa.

4th October 1985

Set off from Kerensa at approximately
3.50 a.m. Had a lift up to the Council
Offices where we boarded the fabulous
Jumbulance to begin our long journey to
Austria.

The Mayor and his wife were there to see
us off. It wasn't long before we were on
our way. My first reaction to the
Jumbulance was that I did not feel as
though I was on board a bus - I honestly
felt as though I was on board a moving
hotel!!

I was treated like a queen right from the
word go, because as soon as I boarded the
bus I was escorted to my bed where I
attempted to have a few hours sleep
without success.

At around 7.00 a.m. I waved to all the
lorry drivers passing by and that was
quite a good laugh - a few of them would
wave back at me!

Our first stop since boarding the bus at
the Council Offices this morning, was in
Bristol. We were due to pick up three
other helpers - one was our doctor called
Ross; Liz, the Chief Nurse, and Audrey,
who was my helper during the course of
the holiday.

On our approach to London the weather
began to turn for the worse; the heavens
really opened - we had our fair share of
fog as well. When we finally arrived in
London the weather was lovely, and Jane

gave us a conducted tour as we were
travelling through the busy streets.

As we progressed towards Dover I decided
to have a lie down on my bed, as I was
still quite tired from getting up at the
crack of dawn this morning. At first I

**ALISON ON BOARD FERRY –
FROM DOVER TO OSTEND**

found it very strange lying down on my
bed while the bus was busily moving along
at top speed, (not quite!) but I enjoyed
it all the same.

It wasn't long before we arrived at the
ferry port at Dover, to begin our ride on
the high seas. Thank goodness it wasn't
too choppy - I didn't particularly want
to be seasick! The crossing from Dover
to Ostend took 4 hours; from 4.15 p.m. to
8.15 p.m. During that time we were all
allowed to get off the bus and go up on
deck.

Due to me being awkward by holding a New
Zealand passport, I was a bit concerned
that I would be questioned and held up
for about an hour! Fortunately Chris,
(one of the drivers) stuck up for me, by
saying that we were all English on board!

Time quickly passed by, and we soon found
ourselves speeding along the straight
wide roads of Belgium.

4th - 5th October 1985

I spent the night on the top bunk right
at the back of the bus, (other folk
complained that I was snoring all night!)
- then I lost my trousers, but that's
another story! I dozed off and when I
woke up I found that I was being
strangled by the seatbelt!

At about 7.10 a.m. I decided to get up.
Not long after that I sat happily having
breakfast speeding through the German
countryside.

Just outside the Austrian boarder I
decided to go to the loo. Jane helped me
on the loo, while Stuart and John waited
outside. On returning to my seat, I
discovered that we had arrived in
Austria.

We had only been in Austria about ten
minutes, when we had already managed to
cause havoc by getting the Jumbulance
stuck under a bridge!!! After Bob, (the
other driver) had managed to get the
Jumbulance out from underneath it,
(ignoring what the police were telling
him to do!) we discovered that a crowd of
people had gathered to watch the sight!!
We then travelled through mountainous
scenery – it was absolutely beautiful,
before arriving at Sport Hotel, St.
Wolfgang Am See at around 12.30 p.m.

"WE'VE FINALLY ARRIVED!!!"

**JUST A FEW OF US SITTING OUTSIDE
THE HOTEL**

**A VERY PLEASANT VIEW
FROM MINE AND AUDREY'S HOTEL ROOM**

**ANOTHER VIEW FROM
OUR HOTEL ROOM**

**AN EXCELLENT VIEW OF
JUMBULANCE MARK 7**

After getting everyone off the Jumbulance and up to their rooms, the lift decided to breakdown - leaving us all stranded on the third floor, with our dinner later waiting for us on the second floor! However, I was escorted by three strong men down the stairs!

Before dinner Audrey, my room-mate, and I had a long sleep till 6.20 p.m. As dinner was at 6.30 p.m., it was a bit of a rush - especially as I had lost my shoes, which eventually turned up under the table!

We had pork, mushrooms, rice, salad and chips for our evening meal; followed by purple ice cream, which was very nice.

After the meal I decided to go to the loo again, but this time, we (Audrey, Ross and I) got trapped in the loo by a gigantic Alsatian dog, which was ready to pounce on us as soon as we came out!!! We managed to get out after he was shut in another room. I thought I heard his paws clawing at the door - but in fact, it was a typewriter!!!

When Audrey, Ross and I had finally managed to leave the loo behind after our little performance with the Alsatian dog, Aud got chattered up by two Austrians who thought she looked like Linda Evans. Then when we eventually arrived back at the bar, Stuart said that the Austrians must have had white sticks if they thought Aud looked like Linda Evans!

We had a couple of drinks, and it wasn't long before we decided to retire for the night by going to bed.

6th October 1985

Audrey and I came down to breakfast at 8.30 a.m. I let my breakfast go down for about five minutes, then we went out on

the veranda and wrote our postcards.
Eileen helped me with most of mine. We
had so many people to write to, postcard
writing took until lunchtime.

Our lunch was very appetizing but I
decided not to eat too much because I
might sink to the bottom of the pool when
I go swimming this afternoon!

I thoroughly enjoyed my swim. As well as
having Jane to help, I had John and
Stuart. After a while I had built up
enough courage to do it on my own.

**AUDREY ALISON EILEEN AND SHIRLEY
ON HOTEL VERANDA**

JANE AND ALISON IN THE HOTEL POOL

114

STUART AND ALISON

**OUR AUDIENCE –
JACK IAN AND MICHAEL**

115

In the evening we all had a get together in the lounge of the hotel. On the way there Stuart was teasing me - I don't quite know how it happened, but as we were coming out of the lift, he decided to present me with a huge flower - which turned out to be plastic!!

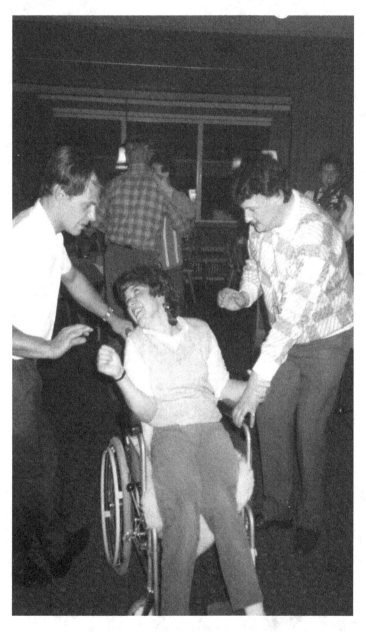

**ALISON DANCING THE NIGHT AWAY
WITH CHRIS AND STUART**

CHRIS AND ALISON FEELING ENERGETIC

It was midnight before I got into bed!

7th October 1985

I awoke this morning to hear Audrey saying that she had broken the bed! Personally I wondered what on earth she was talking about - it turned out that two slats had broken, and she was lying in a hole!!

I was very impressed with what happened
today. On the agenda was a trip to the
Hellbrunn Water Gardens and Salzburg.

I thought the Water Gardens were
absolutely remarkable. We were told by
the Austrian Tourist Guide that the
person who invented the Water Gardens had
a very funny sense of humour. It
certainly turned out that way because
everywhere that we seemed to walk - no
doubt about it, we would be sprayed with
water!!

LIZ AND CHRIS IN THE WATER GARDENS

AN AMAZING PLACE

WATER THEATRE

WATER TUNNEL

When it was time to leave the Water
Gardens, we all had to go through a water
tunnel to get out - that was a real
laugh!! After we had dried off, we
decided to have a picnic lunch not far
from the Jumbulance.

THE BEAUTIFUL CITY OF SALZBURG

Later on we drove to Salzburg, where we
split up into small groups. In my group
I had, Audrey, Eileen, Shirley, Liz and
John.

**"THIS HOT CHOCOLATE
IS HIGHLY RECOMMENDED!!"**

To begin with, we all decided to taste Austrian Hot Chocolate – it was absolutely beautiful. While drinking our chocolate we noticed horses trotting by pulling carts, so, after making enquires, all of us except John, decided to have a ride. John was left looking after the wheelchairs.

**A PROUD AUSTRIAN
WITH HIS LOVELY HORSES**

**SHIRLEY AND ALISON
ALMOST READY TO GO!!**

"A GREAT PHOTO SHEILA!!!"

Audrey, Shirley, Liz, Eileen and I had a lovely ride around the old part of Salzburg. During our journey we met up with Sheila. Sheila was so surprised when she saw us - she **had** to run along behind and get a photo of us all!!

When we eventually arrived back at our starting point - not only was John still guarding the wheelchairs, he was also dying to go to the loo. So, there we all were frantically running around Salzburg, trying to find a loo for poor old John!!

In the evening I had a very relaxing time writing my diary and talking to John and Stuart in the lounge on the second floor of the hotel.

8th October 1985

Had a very scenic day today as we travelled by Jumbulance viewing the five lakes surrounding St. Wolfgang. I think the scenery in Austria is absolutely out of this world – I would love to bring Mum and Dad here one day.

For the majority of the journey I decided to lie down on my top bunk and relax for a while. Stuart and John offered to lift me up there.

In the afternoon we found a lovely hotel with a fantastic view – I was very impressed with it. Even though it wasn't opening hours, the hotel owner kindly invited us all in for a drink.

PENSION HOTEL

I must admit that I was feeling slightly
light-headed when it was time to leave,
because I had drunk about five glasses of
wine!!! The Austrians don't serve wine
by the glass - they serve it by the jug,
and I felt that I couldn't waste the
contents of the jug - it was only
small!!!

On the way back to our hotel - because of
my present state, I asked to be lifted up
on my top bunk - I slept soundly!!

In the evening we had our "Tramps and
Tarts" fancy dress party - there were
some really funny sights around!!! I
would love to know what the Austrians
thought of us that night!!!

AUDREY ALISON AND JOHN

BOOGIE STUART!!

**"I WILL CERTAINLY GET A MAN
DRESSED LIKE THIS!!!"**

125

"DAVE HAS FOUND TWO NICE BIRDS!!!"

BOB AND CHRIS!!!
(JUMBULANCE DRIVERS)

After dancing with just about every man on the dance floor, (apart from the Austrians!) I managed to make it to bed at about 2.15 a.m.!!

AUSTRIAN DANCERS

9th October 1985

Before lunch I went into town with Audrey and Ross. I managed to do a bit of shopping before discovering a restaurant that had some absolutely lovely food in it, and we couldn't resist experiencing the taste - so much so that I could not eat my lunch!

Went back to the hotel just to have a
drink - Ross and I were then out on the
town once more! I was running short of
money so we decided to go to the nearest
bank to cash some travellers cheques.
Whilst in the bank, we noticed something
very strange - there was bread on
display!!

Ross and I couldn't be too long in town,
because at 2.45 p.m. we were due to hit
the high seas! I spent most of my time
up on deck viewing the sights and trying
to act like David Bailey the second!!

ALISON AND DAVE ON BOARD THE BOAT

After surviving the boat trip; and not
feeling too seasick (I'm becoming quite a
good sailor!) - in the evening I sat in
the lounge of the hotel, listened to some
music and talked to John, (the helper)
before going off to bed.

10th October 1985

Boarded the Jumbulance at 9.45 a.m. I
must admit that I was feeling very

excited about going up the Dachstein mountain in a cable car today!

When we arrived at the mountainside, my feelings soon changed! I felt guilty because I had forced John to come up with me, but he didn't want to as he thought he was going to be ill. The tables had turned though – I felt a lot worse than John did!!

JOHN AND ALISON INSIDE THE CABLE CAR

"UP WE GO!!!"

"THE GROUND BENEATH US!!!"

**A FOGGY VIEW FROM THE MOUNTAIN TOP –
"WE MADE IT!!!"**

**SHEILA AT THE TOP OF THE
DACHSTEIN MOUNTAIN WAVING THE
CORNISH FLAG!!!**

11th October 1985

Boarded the Jumbulance at our usual time
of 9.45 a.m. Today we were due to visit
Eagle's Nest, which was quite a long way
from our hotel in St. Wolfgang.

Very much to our disappointment – having
arrived at Eagle's Nest, we discovered
that we couldn't actually get inside. We
could only view it from on board the
Jumbulance.

After spending about half an hour in the
car park, with everybody around admiring
the bus, we decided to set off again,
towards Salzburg; where we had lunch
arranged in a hotel. Spaghetti was on
the menu – that was extremely difficult
to eat – I got more on the floor than in
my mouth!!

The afternoon was spent sightseeing and
shopping for presents. We were told to
be back at the bus for 5.45 p.m. but I

didn't arrive until 5.55 p.m. as John,
Stuart and I got lost in the middle of
Salzburg!!

Later on we had a farewell party because
tonight is our last night in Austria
before we all board the Jumbulance again
tomorrow night, to begin our 37 hour
journey home.

12th October 1985

Didn't do a lot this morning apart from
help Audrey and Ross pack my suitcase. I
then went down to the dining room and
spoke to Mike and Manuella until dinner
time.

In the afternoon we had a rather wet
journey going up the side of a mountain
behind our village - by train.

It was 8.30 p.m. when we reluctantly left
St. Wolfgang behind us, and began our
long ride home. I spent the night on the
top bunk lying directly behind Chris and
Bob.

13th October 1985

I slept for practically the whole night,
apart from being turned over by Pat and
Stuart. When I woke up properly at 7.00
a.m. we were driving through Belgium.

After a few more hours of travelling we
arrived at Ostend ferry port, but didn't
actually sail until just after 2.00 p.m.
Our sailing was very pleasant, and even
though the sea was quite calm, the ferry
was rolling slightly.

When we had been sailing for quite a
while, Stuart, John and Chris came up to
me and said, "We've got a surprise for
you." I discovered that they had
arranged for me to go up on the bridge of
the ferry to meet the captain! The

captain was a very nice man - he told us
a story about an Irish man jumping
overboard just 3 days ago!!

'CAPTAIN' ALISON!!

It wasn't long before we were all on
board the Jumbulance again to begin our
final stretch home. The last few hours
on the Jumbulance were very tearful, as
we all found it very very difficult to
say goodbye to each other.

That was a holiday that I shall never
ever forget - thank you everybody.

BRIDE ALISON
THURSDAY 1ST OCTOBER 1987

CHAPTER SIX

"I ALISON, TAKE YOU, LAWRENCE"

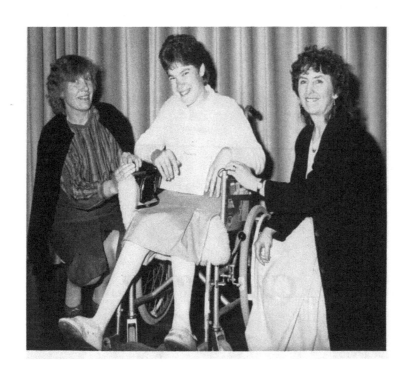

**PHOTO COURTESY OF BERNARD WHITE/
CORNISH GUARDIAN NEWSPAPER**

KATE ALISON AND MARY
9TH MAY 1986

When I first arrived at Kerensa I was told that I would only be staying for a maximum of three months. Those three months were extremely long, as my actual time at Kerensa - from start to finish, turned out to be 2½ years!! Not only was I able to continue with my education, I was also taught how to cope with general life skills - i.e. living independently. "Many thanks to everybody involved - your help and encouragement has done me the power of good."

On Friday 9th May 1986, my achievements at Mid Cornwall College were formally recognised. I attended a presentation evening with several of my fellow students, tutors, family and friends. I have to say that I felt extremely chuffed with myself when I was awarded the top college award - the J M Oades Memorial Award - for overall diligence in the 1984-85 academic year.

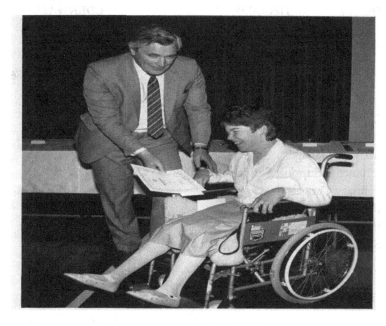

PHOTO COURTESY OF BERNARD WHITE/
CORNISH GUARDIAN NEWSPAPER

A PROUD MOMENT FOR ALISON
9TH MAY 1986

During my time living independently in one of the bungalows within the grounds of Kerensa - one afternoon while I was having a general sort out, I suddenly became very excited!! I had discovered Larry McGovern's address within a National Star Centre Old Students Magazine. I was so keen to get back in touch with Larry - I sent him a postcard.

Having now completed my studies - as well as concentrating on my independent living skills, I was also very keen to find employment - that proved to be a challenge and a half!! A letter given to me following an interview read:-

CORNWALL AND ISLES OF SCILLY HEALTH AUTHORITY
MENTAL HEALTH UNIT

Telephone:	*BODMIN 3281*	*ST. LAWRENCE'S HOSPITAL*
		BODMIN
Our Ref:	HFG/ALP	*CORNWALL*
		PL31 2QT
Your Ref:		

12 December 1986

If you Telephone please ask for: Ext 2323

Mr Paul Hanage
Finance & Support Services Manager
Primary Care Unit
Penrice Hospital
Porthpean Road
ST AUSTELL

Dear Paul

As I believe you have recently assumed responsibility for Personnel management in the Primary Care Unit, I am writing to you concerning a young lady whom I had the pleasure of interviewing for a secretarial post on Tuesday.

Her name is Alison Kerr and she is 20 years old. The post for which she had applied is that of Personal Secretary to the Clinical Psychologist in Medical Rehabilitation based at Blantyre Hostel. Unfortunately, she was rather inexperienced for that post and we appointed another candidate.

However she would make an excellent copy typist/office junior as her appearance, attitude and determination are very impressive. She is highly self-motivated and would be an asset to a General office or department where she would not have to assume full responsibility.

The reason for my going to this trouble is that Miss Kerr suffers from cerebral palsy and is confined to a wheelchair (although she can walk with the aid of support, even negotiating stairs successfully). She has no speech impediment and is a bright, well educated young lady who deserves a chance at steady employment.

She has her own transport, and works one day a week for Restormel Borough Council who are delighted with her.

Do you think you might have some vacancy in the area which she may be suitable to fill? I feel strongly that she deserves an opportunity to work in a paid job, and that as Managers in a caring organisation like the NHS we should do all we can to help.

I would be glad to have her here but the distance of 10 miles each way, certainly in bad weather would be a distinct drawback to her.

If you would like further information please contact Betty Skidmore, Clinical Psychologist at Blantyre, who interviewed Alison with me.

Yours sincerely

Helen Gough

H F Gough (Miss)
Manager General Services & Personnel

cc: Mr D Green
    Mr M Fletcher
    Mrs B Skidmore

**VIEW OF HOSTEL AND WORK UNIT
FROM LOWER BUNGALOW
KERENSA**

You may be slightly surprised to learn that my method of transport mentioned in Helen's letter, was in fact a 50cc motorbike!!!! Driving it while sitting in either my manual or electric wheelchair was certainly an experience. The summer months were good fun, but any other time was a different story. The exact date escapes me, but on the day I collected it from Truro, following an intense driving lesson, the weather was atrocious. When I arrived back at Kerensa, I must have looked like a drowned rat! I had just driven through a severe thunderstorm – never again!!! Buying a motorbike wasn't one of my best assets – I much prefer four wheels, a roof and not having to wear a crash helmet!!

**BACK AND FRONT VIEW OF
'NIPPI' 50CC MOTORBIKE**

ALISON MUM DAD AND VERA

Staying on the subject of transport, my renewed desire for independent travel came about after attending an all day driving assessment (again in Truro) on Thursday 16th May 1985. I was a guest of the Banstead Place Mobility Centre. To be given the opportunity to get behind the wheel again and actually drive around Truro was just fantastic, as I hadn't driven since my student days in Cheltenham. I was so happy!!

BEAMING ALISON!!!

Looking back at my time at Kerensa, I certainly achieved an awful lot in those 2½ years – studying at a mainstream college, living independently, meeting people and having loads of fun.

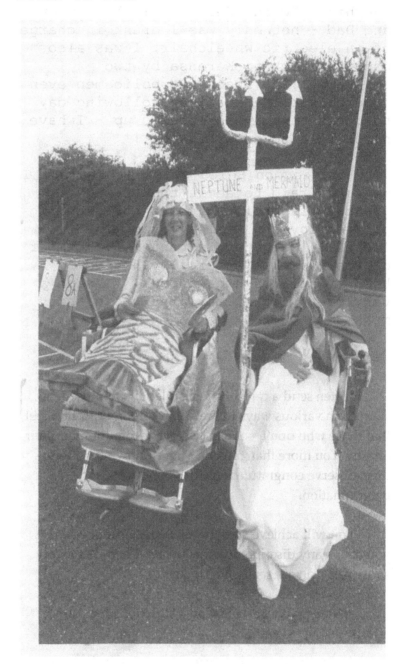

PHOTO COURTESY OF BERNARD WHITE/
CORNISH GUARDIAN NEWSPAPER

**ALISON AND SYLVIA
TAKING PART IN THE ST AUSTELL CARNIVAL!!!**

I even had a brush with the law!!!
On my nineteenth birthday, after
consuming a fair amount of alcohol in
The Western Pub in St. Austell, I wasn't
capable of driving my electric
wheelchair in a straight line back up
the hill towards Kerensa!!! "Sorry Mum
and Dad – not only was I drunk in charge
of an electric wheelchair, I was also
escorted back to Kerensa by two
policemen!!!" Those two policemen even
came back to Kerensa the following day
to check that I had sobered up – I have
never felt so embarrassed!!!!

Focusing on Helen's letter again. I
am not afraid to admit that I was
greatly disappointed about not securing
paid employment whilst living in St.
Austell. Margaret Carpenter – a member
of the hostel staff really helped to
keep my spirits high though. Inside a
very pretty card, Margaret wrote this
message:–

Dear Ali,

I often send a card of congratulations to those who
succeed in various ways in life. But more important, I feel
that those who don't, equally deserve recognition for their
efforts. You more than anyone I have known for a long
time, deserve congratulations for your efforts and
determination.

You will achieve strength of character that will rise
you above any disappointments in life. Keep that lovely
smile Ali. You are really nice to know.

With Best Wishes and Congratulations for your
efforts.

Margaret C.

"Thank you so much Margaret."

I can hear you asking, "When is she going to put me in the picture with regard to what happened after Larry's postcard was sent to him?" "Thank you for your patience – that moment has now arrived!!"

Shortly after sending Larry's postcard, I was called to the hostel office to receive a phone call. Very much to my surprise, it was Larry!! I couldn't believe my ears – to hear Larry's voice again was absolutely fantastic. I was over the moon!!! Larry's feelings were the same, but unfortunately I cannot repeat what he said when my postcard was received!!!

For several months Larry and I kept both British Telecom and British Rail in business – if we weren't taking it in turns to travel from one side of the country to the other, we would spend hours talking on the phone, literally!!

I thoroughly enjoyed travelling on my own by train to visit Larry. Obviously my journey began at St. Austell railway station. Upon leaving St. Austell I would travel to London Paddington. I then had to catch a connecting train from London Kings Cross to Huntingdon, in Cambridgeshire – where Larry would meet me. How did I travel from London Paddington to London Kings Cross? In a London black cab. On one occasion the driver said to me, "What are you doing travelling through London on your own, in your situation?" I replied, "I'm on my way to visit my boyfriend who lives near Cambridge – we're getting engaged soon." I must have made the taxi driver's day – he gave me a free fare!

**LARRY OUTSIDE LOWER BUNGALOW
AT KERENSA**

At the stroke of midnight on
Saturday, 14th February, (the most
romantic day of the year – St.
Valentine's Day) 1987, Larry knelt down
on one knee, and, just as he asked that
mega important question, "Will you marry
me?" – Larry lost his balance and fell
over! A few minutes later – feeling
very emotional, but with absolutely no
hesitation, I said, "Yes – of course I
will."

To celebrate our engagement our friends and family joined Larry and I at Kerensa for a very enjoyable and memorable party during the evening of St. Valentine's Day. I couldn't stop showing off my sapphire and diamond ring!!

**ALISON AND LARRY
CHATTING WITH KATE AND GWENDA**

**CUTTING OUR ENGAGEMENT CAKE
MADE BY HOSTEL COOK – ANNE**

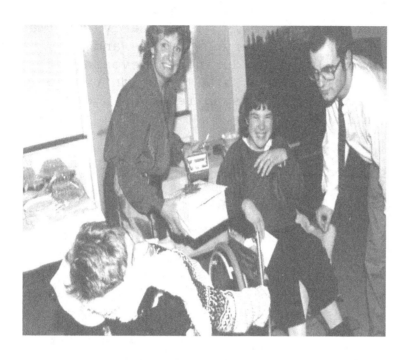

**GIFT RECEIVING WITH
BARBARA AND COLIN ROSTRON**

**ALISON – DETERMINED TO JOIN EVERYONE
ON THE DANCE FLOOR**

148

**ALISON STANDING WITH HER
NEW FIANCÈ LARRY**

During the disco I dedicated The
Power of Love - by Jennifer Rush, to
Larry. Not only do I like the tune -
the lyrics made me feel that I'm talking
to Larry.

"The whispers in the morning
Of lovers sleeping tight
Are rolling like thunder now
As I look in your eyes

I hold on to your body
And feel each move you make
Your voice is warm and tender
A love I cannot forsake

Cause I'm your lady
And you are my man
Whenever you reach for me
I'll do all that I can

(Lost is how I'm feeling
lying in your arms
When the world outside
Is too much to take
That all ends when I'm with you)

Even though there may be times
It seems I'm far away
Never wonder where I am
Cause I am always by your side

Cause I'm your lady
And you are my man
Whenever you reach for me
I'll do all that I can

We're heading for something
Somewhere I've never been
Sometimes I am frightened
But I'm ready to learn
About the power of love

150

The sound of your heart beating
Made it clear suddenly
The feeling that I can't go on
Is light years away

Cause I'm your lady
And you are my man
Whenever you reach for me
I'll do all that I can

We're heading for something
Somewhere I've never been
Sometimes I am frightened
But I'm ready to learn
About the power of love"

In April 1987 – as a consequence of
our recent engagement, I received a card
of congratulations from my Nana, in New
Zealand. Including a lovely note
written by Nana, it read:-

On Your Engagement

To my dear Ali & your fiancé, this is wonderful news,

It's grand when
nice things happen
And that's especially true
When the happy news
is centred around
Two people fine as you –
So enjoy the busy hours
Your engagement's
sure to bring
And may life hold

for both of you
The best of everything!

Bless you both, Congratulations and much love from Nana Kerr x x x x

26th March   11 AM here in N.Z.

Aunty Helen has just told me she has been talking to Mum and Julia &
that you are getting married in October, this is wonderful for you. Do write &
tell me all about this dear man whom you have found & vice versa. How old is
he, dark or fair & all about what you both do & to where you are going to live.

Lovely news my dear, I am so happy for you.

Love Nana. x x x x

Larry and I certainly did enjoy the
busy hours our engagement brought. At
roughly the same time that Nana wrote
that card, I was preparing to leave
Kerensa to begin my new life in
Cambridgeshire with Larry. We just
couldn't bear to be apart from now on!

My departure from Kerensa happened
almost overnight - once I set my mind on
something, and it is within my
capabilities - I go ahead and do it!
With Larry's help I moved all my
belongings (excluding my NIPPI motorbike
and electric wheelchair - that was
transported at a later date) from
Cornwall to Cambridgeshire - by train!!!
The reaction we received when Larry and
I arrived at Huntingdon Railway Station
was unforgettable!!! "Christ Bill,
they've got everything here apart from
the bloody kitchen sink!!!" That was
true, as several suitcases, my walking
frame and Hazel (my cat, in her pet-
carrier) were lined up along the
platform!!! Larry even had to ask
whether he could store some of my stuff
at the station overnight, as he couldn't
fit it all in his mini!!

LARRY AND HIS 'MAD' MINI!!

Our accommodation in St. Neots,
Cambridgeshire, was by no means suitable
for our needs, but Larry and I were
happy to put up with anything in order
to stay together. My cat Hazel was not
happy with her new surroundings though –
sadly, she ran away.

In the summer of 1987 – thanks to
the Woman's Royal Voluntary Service,
Larry and I were chuffed when we were
asked to sign a tenancy agreement for a
purpose-built ground floor, one-bedroom
flat – part of a new housing development
situated in Cambridge. We also had 24
hour back up from a residential warden –
this was very reassuring.

By the middle of September, all the arrangements and preparations for our wedding day on Thursday 1st October had been finalised – I even practised my new signature several times over!!

On the morning of Wednesday 30th September, Larry left home to spend his last few hours of freedom over at Papworth Everard. Apparently he was extremely nervous – our friend Tim Bingham will no doubt agree with that!! I have to say that I felt more excited than nervous – I kept thinking to myself, "I'm getting married in the morning!!"

Larry and I could not have been luckier with the weather on our special day if we'd tried – it was absolutely beautiful.

**PATRICK MARTIN AND GWENDA ARRIVING AT
ST ANDREW'S CHURCH CHESTERTON CAMBRIDGE
"I WORKED WITH MARTIN AND GWENDA AT
THE COUNCIL OFFICES IN ST AUSTELL"**

**ALISON WITH HER BRIDESMAIDS –
JULIA AND VANESSA**

MISS ALISON ANN KERR

From the minute I woke up on my
wedding day I was really eager to get to
church to show my dress and myself off
to everybody - especially Larry. "Helen
- thank you so much for travelling
12,000 miles from New Zealand to help
your niece with her make-up!!!"

**HERE COMES THE BRIDE –
ALISON**

Despite my eagerness, Dad and I
arrived at church 15 minutes late!!
Larry and Reverend Carrè had become
rather restless - Barry (Larry's
brother) had also shouted out, "Right,
she's not coming - she's changed her
mind!!!"

Very much to Larry and Reverend
Carrè's relief, I had certainly not
changed my mind! Seeing Reverend Carrè
standing at the church door, I didn't
want to waste anymore time. Upon
entering the inside of St. Andrew's -
the first person that caught my
attention was my brother Pete. Pete was
given the job of ushering all our guests
to their seats.

The organist had obviously received
the signal that Dad and I had arrived,
as suddenly the tune 'Here Comes The
Bride' could be heard loud and clear
throughout the church. As Dad and I
were moving down the aisle - not only
did I have a huge smile on my face - I
thought, "This tune is being played
especially for me. I'm the bride!!"

Larry's first words to me when I
arrived at his side were, "You look
beautiful."

Reverend Carrè was soon conducting
our marriage service. Saying my
marriage vows to Larry was a very
serious, but also a very special
experience - and I can honestly say that
I meant every word.

Within what seemed like only a few
minutes, Reverend Carrè proclaimed that
Larry and I were now husband and wife.
At that moment I felt as though my
happiness couldn't get any better - I
knew that Larry was now officially my

husband — nobody could take him away —
he's mine!! Reverend Carrè then handed
me our marriage certificate saying,

"Enjoy your life sentence!!"

At the age of 21, I suddenly felt
very grown up.

To conclude the service we all sang
my favourite hymn:-

NOW THANK WE ALL OUR GOD

Now thank we all our God,
with hearts and hands and
voices,
Who wondrous things has
done, in whom this world
rejoices;
Who from our mothers' arms
has blessed us on our way
With countless gifts of love,
and still is ours today.
O may this bounteous God
through all our life be near us,
With ever joyful hearts and
blessed peace to cheer us;
And keep still in grace, and
guide us when perplexed;
And free us from all ills, in this
world and the next.

*All praise and thanks to God
the Father now be given;
The Son and Him Who reigns
with Them in highest heaven;
The one eternal God, Whom
earth and heaven adore;
For thus it was, is now, and
shall be evermore.*

Words by Martin Rinkart (1586-1649)

I am sure that Dad will not mind me mentioning that all the way through that final hymn, Dad was quite tearful. He has always denied the fact, (possibly through embarrassment) but I promise you - I know what I heard!! "Rest assured Dad - you may have given your daughter away in marriage - Larry will always be my husband, but you will never lose me totally. You will always be my Dad."

**ALISON LARRY BARRY
JULIA AND VANESSA**

ALISON JULIA AND VANESSA

**MR AND MRS
LAWRENCE CHRISTOPHER GERARD
McGOVERN**

ALISON AND LARRY
(WITH GRAND-DAD WALSH CLOSE BY)

Following our wedding ceremony at
St. Andrew's Church in Chesterton,
Cambridge - as a newly married couple,
Larry and I were chauffeur driven (as I
was with Dad to church) 15 miles, to the
Village Hall in Papworth Everard. With
all our guests following closely behind
us - Larry and I felt like royalty!!

161

"A TOAST TO THE BRIDE AND GROOM"
(WAS QUITE OFTEN SAID)!!

Our wedding was quite an
international affair! Guests travelled
from New Zealand, Germany and America –
as well as from various counties in
England – for example, Devon, Cornwall,
Merseyside and Kent. I mustn't forget
to mention Cambridgeshire too!

**"CUTTING A WEDDING CAKE
IS HARD WORK!!!"**

A poem called 'A Good Wedding Cake'
by Noreen Littleton, was written on a
notelet to Larry and I - sent by our
friend Thelma Lashmore. Thelma was
distraught when she had to refuse our
wedding invitation.

BRIDEGROOM LARRY

BRIDE ALISON
(WITH HER EYES CLOSED)!!

DAD MAKING HIS SPEECH
"WHAT IS HE SAYING? – SADLY I CANNOT REMEMBER"

AN EMOTIONAL HUG
WITH MUM-IN-LAW JOAN

I thoroughly enjoyed every minute of our wedding day, and wore my wedding dress until gone midnight!

The evening was spent back in Cambridge – being led on a mini pub-crawl by Larry's Grand-dad – he had a great sense of humour!! We all must have looked an absolute picture on Chesterton Road, heading towards The Old Spring, and ending up in the Portland Arms. Grand-dad Walsh also kept saying, "Show us your garter." I gave in, in the end!!

Another person with a great sense of humour was my new brother-in-law Barry. He had only secretly filled our bed with an enormous amount of confetti!!! Larry and I were discovering confetti in our home for months afterwards – "thank you Barry!!!"

**FIRST CLASS TRAIN TRAVEL FOR ALISON
(AND HER NEW HUSBAND LARRY)**

**THE ARGYLL HOTEL
IN DUNOON – SCOTLAND**

During our ten day honeymoon in
Dunoon, the weather wasn't much to be
desired – it was pretty wet and cold –
who worries about the weather while on
honeymoon anyway?!!

Larry and I couldn't thank the staff
enough at the Argyll Hotel. On our
arrival chilled bottled champagne and
flowers greeted us in our room, and
everybody concerned made our stay
extremely comfortable and enjoyable.

"Thank you so much for asking me to
be your wife Larry - I love you - and I
always will."

CHAPTER SEVEN

"YOU'RE BETTER OFF TALKING TO BARCLAYS"

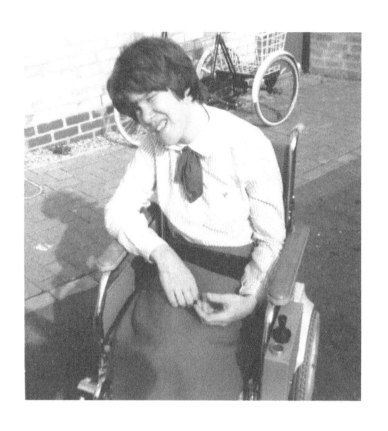

"THANK YOU BARCLAYS"

14TH MARCH 1988 –
9TH MAY 2002

"YOU'RE BETTER OFF TALKING TO BARCLAYS"

The practising of my new signature soon brought me good luck! Larry and I had only been married for a matter of weeks, when a letter from the JobCentre - addressed to me, landed on our doormat.

9TH NOV 1987

Mrs A. McGovern

JOBCENTRE
Guildhall Chambers
Guildhall Place
Cambridge
CB2 3QU

Tel 64941

Ext 45

Dear Alison,

A job has arisen in Histon for a telephonist/receptionist with some typing duties. The employer has asked us if there are any interested disabled people.

The job is due to start on 14th December. I shall send you an application form as soon as I receive them. Please ring me if you would like to know more details.

Yours Sincerely,

Neil Brook

N.F. Brook
Manpower Services Commission Employment Division

```
    It goes without saying - I was
without a doubt, interested - I was
delighted! Within days I received a
letter from Barclays:-
```

BARCLAYS BANK PLC

Local Head Office

P.O. Box No. 2, 15 Bene't Street, Cambridge CB2 3PZ

Telephone: (0223) 315315

All communications to be addressed to the Local Directors

Mrs A McGovern
3 Coach House Court
Hawthorn Way
CAMBRIDGE
CB4 1BT

19 November 1987

DAS/SH

Dear Mrs McGovern

We are presently considering our staffing needs for our new
Regional Office at Histon and have a vacancy for a
telephonist/receptionist. We understand from Mrs Gellert at the
Cambridge Job Centre that you might be interested and
therefore enclose an application form herewith. If you would
like to be considered in competition with others would you be
kind enough to complete this and return it to this address as
soon as possible.

Yours very truly

David Starr

D A STARR
PERSONNEL MANAGER

Enc.

Registered in London, England. Reg. No: 1026167. Reg. Office: 54 Lombard Street, London EC3P 3AH

I completed the application form as
fast as I possibly could - and upon
returning it, the postman delivered yet
another letter addressed to me from
Barclays! Goodness knows what he
thought!!

BARCLAYS BANK PLC

Local Head Office

P.O. Box No. 2, 15 Bene't Street, Cambridge CB2 3PZ

Telephone: (0223) 315315

All communications to be addressed to the Local Directors

Mrs A A McGovern
3 Coach House Court
Hawthorn Way
CAMBRIDGE
CB4 1BT

27 November 1987

MG/SH

Dear Mrs McGovern

Thank you for completing our staff application form. We have a
number of applicants to consider and have made a tentative
appointment for you for Thursday next, 3 December at 2.30 pm
at our Market Hill, Cambridge branch.

You should have no difficulty in getting there since there is a
ramp up to the main entrance and also an automatically opening
door. However, if you feel there could be a problem, please do
not hesitate to contact us when we will endeavour to make
alternative arrangements.

Yours sincerely

M Gardiner

M GARDINER (MRS)
PERSONNEL ASSISTANT

Registered in London, England. Reg. No: 1026167. Reg. Office: 54 Lombard Street, London EC3P 3AH

"I'll take you via Silver Street" were the words of the taxi driver as we were travelling to my interview on that Thursday afternoon - 3rd December 1987.

Wheelchair access at Barclays Cambridge, Market Hill branch proved to be no problem - "Excellent," I thought.

I felt my interview with David Starr went very well, and I was soon put at ease. Obviously David had several questions for me to answer (he seemed to have loads of paper on the desk in front of him)! I had one or two questions for David too:-

"Where in Histon is Regional Office situated?"
"Does the building have ramped access?"
"Does the building have a lift?"
"Are there toilet facilities for disabled people?"

When David answered (very positively) "Yes" to my second, third and fourth question, I immediately thought - "I might be in with a chance here."

At the end of my interview David kindly saw me to my taxi, which was parked not far from the branch. Before saying our goodbyes - David said, "I'll be in touch."

I was feeling very pleased with myself going home in the taxi.

Christmas and New Years Eve went by. Larry returned to his job at Papworth Everard and, I was still unemployed - eagerly wanting to know the outcome of my interview.

On Wednesday 6th January 1988 our postman was back to his usual duties too

- a letter from Barclays was once again waiting on our doormat for me. Extremely nervously, I opened it - scared stiff of disappointment. After reading David's letter twice over, I suddenly shrieked with absolute delight! Our cat Candy must have thought, "My god, she's gone mad!!!" (I'll tell you about Candy in more detail later on).

Once I had returned to my senses - I replied to David's letter as requested. I honestly couldn't believe my luck - **"thank you so much David** - it took me ages to touch down on earth again, I can tell you!!"

BARCLAYS

BARCLAYS BANK PLC
Cambridge Regional Office
P.O. Box No. 90, Histon, Cambridge CB4 4ZX
Telephone: Histon (022 023) 2133

All communications to be addressed to the Regional
Your Ref:
Our Ref:
Ext. No:

Mrs A A McGovern
3 Coach House Court
Hawthorn Way
CAMBRIDGE
CB4 1BT

5 January 1988

DAS/SH

Dear Mrs McGovern

You will know by now of my telephone conversation with Mrs Gellert who will have spoken to you herself by telephone. I am writing firstly to advise you that the vacancy of telephonist/receptionist for which I interviewed you has for the time being been filled. However, I wondered if you would be interested in undertaking typing and other general duties on a trial basis for say a 4-6 week period subject to an assessment being made of any additional equipment which may have to be provided to enable you to deal with audio typing duties.

If you would be interested perhaps you would be kind enough to write to me and let me know so that arrangements may be made as quickly as possible.

Yours very truly

D A STARR
PERSONNEL MANAGER

Facsimile: (022 023) 2159
Registered in London, England. Reg. No: 1026167. Reg. Office: 54 Lombard Street, London EC3P 3AH

```
They say that good things come to
those that wait, and wait is exactly
what I did!!! Then, very much to my
relief, this letter arrived:-
```

BARCLAYS BANK PLC
Cambridge Regional Office
P.O. Box No. 90, Mortlock House, Histon, Cambridge CB4 4ZX
Telephone: (022 023) 2133

Mrs A A McGovern   Your Ref:
3 Coach House Court   Our Ref:
Hawthorn Way   Ext:
CAMBRIDGE
CB4 1BT

23 February 1988

MFB/SH

Dear Alison

No doubt you are wondering how we are progressing with your
employment with ourselves and a start date.

We can now inform you that all the formalities have been
completed and we are simply waiting for the downstairs toilet to
be finished which we hope will be very shortly.

In the meantime, keep patient and we will be contacting you as
quickly as possible.

Kind regards.

Yours sincerely

M F Batt

M F BATT
PERSONNEL ASSISTANT

Facsimile: (022 023) 2159
Registered in London, England. Reg. No: 1026167. Reg. Office: 54 Lombard Street, London EC3P 3AH

"Keeping patient was extremely difficult Mike!! I was soon lifted back up on cloud nine though – after reading your next letter":-

BARCLAYS BANK PLC
Cambridge Regional Office
P.O. Box No. 90, Mortlock House, Histon, Cambridge CB4 4ZX
Telephone: (022 023) 2133

Mrs A A McGovern   Your Ref:
3 Coach House Court   Our Ref:
Hawthorn Way   Ext:
CAMBRIDGE
CB4 1BT

1 March 1988

MFB/SH

Dear Alison

Good news! The downstairs toilet facilities are now operational and therefore we can arrange for you to join us here in Histon.

We suggest that you start on Monday, 14 March, say at 10.00 am.

We look forward to seeing you then but, in the meantime, should you have any questions to ask please do not hesitate to contact us.

Kind regards.

Yours sincerely

M F Batt

M F BATT
PERSONNEL ASSISTANT

Facsimile: (022 023) 2159
Registered in London, England. Reg. No: 1026167. Reg. Office: 54 Lombard Street, London EC3P 3AH

ALISON –
VERY HAPPY TO BE A MEMBER OF
CAMBRIDGE REGIONAL OFFICE
SECRETARIAL TEAM

Alison

Just a short note to congratulate you on your appointment to the permanent staff.

It is greatly deserved and you are an asset to Barclays staff.

I'm off on holiday for 2 weeks now but look forward to seeing your smiling face when I return.

Kind Regards

Diane
x

Not long after Diane very kindly sent me that note, I was asking my supervisor Viv, for some holiday too – to attend Julia's wedding on Saturday 14th May.

NANA KERR

ALISON AND LARRY

I smiled a lot on Julia's wedding
day - but, during the night before -
also cried a lot. I was very happy
about Julia getting married, but
absolutely distraught that Julia was now
beginning her new life in America. How
often would we see each other? My twin
sister was no longer living in the same
country as me - saying goodbye to Julia
was immensely difficult.

Spending time with Larry and I in
Cambridge – after Julia's wedding, Nana
Kerr was another person that I had to
say goodbye to, very tearfully. Minutes
before Nana left in a taxi – to begin
her long flight back to New Zealand,
Nana said to me, "When will I see you
back in New Zealand my dear?" My reply
was, "I can't honestly say when it will
be – but, **I promise you**, you will see me
back in New Zealand one day."

CHAPTER EIGHT

THE UPS AND DOWNS OF PREGNANCY

"YES –
IT'S POSITIVE!!!
I'M PREGNANT!!!"

The thought of me becoming a Mum was just wonderful – I wanted to shout my news from the rooftops there and then!! I was so happy.

After having my pregnancy confirmed by my doctor, Dr. Robson – I couldn't resist telling people my good news – especially my supervisor at work – Viv. I also couldn't stay out of Mothercare!!

Christmas 1988 was fast approaching – Larry and I were feeling very happy with ourselves – we had recently bought a cot for Baby McGovern – Jan Young (our Health Visitor) had introduced herself to us – and my scan appointment at the Rosie Maternity Hospital (situated on the same site as Addenbrooke's Hospital) had been booked for me.

"Oh my god" – that was my reaction whilst in the disabled toilet at work on the afternoon of Tuesday 13th December. After seeing blood – padding myself up as quickly as I could, I discreetly called Viv downstairs. "I'm bleeding – I've got to go home," I said.

As soon as Larry and I arrived back at home – the doctor was called, and I was advised to have total bed rest. Reverend Lorna Dazeley also visited, and did her utmost in providing me with some much-needed words of comfort.

Sadly, on Wednesday 14th December, the inevitable happened – at exactly 12 weeks into my pregnancy I suffered a miscarriage – I was utterly devastated.

During my journey to the Rosie Maternity Hospital by ambulance, Larry was very much in my thoughts – I felt desperately sorry for him. Not only had Larry witnessed his wife losing our baby – he also had to clean up the evidence left behind in our bathroom.

Lying in my bed on Lady Mary Ward – listening to the cries of newborn babies, broke my heart. I was thinking, "Why have they put me here? I have just lost my baby."

Needless to say, Christmas 1988 in our household was by no means a happy one. I just could not stop crying – I kept blaming myself for our loss – asking questions like, "What if I hadn't done this?" "Perhaps I should have done that?"

Larry and I were determined not to give up trying for a family as we both wanted to become parents so badly. Our doctor advised us to wait at least a couple of months, before trying again.

**BEAUTIFUL FLOWERS
RECEIVED FROM MY COLLEAGUES
AT BARCLAYS**

IT'S
A GIRL!

EMMA LOUISE

ARRIVED AT 6.28 P.M. ON
THURSDAY 13TH SEPTEMBER 1990
WEIGHING 7LB 9OZS!

Happy Birthday!

CHAPTER NINE

A BIG WELCOME TO LITTLE EMMA LOUISE

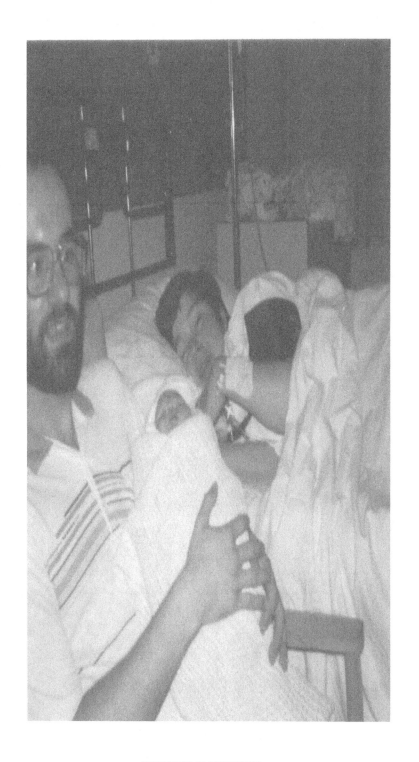

**PROUD PARENTS –
ALISON AND LARRY
WITH NEWBORN BABY
EMMA LOUISE**

"So you're ready to face the world again Als"
were the exact words Faith said whilst
walking through reception, seeing me at
work behind the desk.

   Yes - I was very pleased to be back
at Regional Office with all my friends -
looking to the future.

   My first Performance Appraisal
Report read:-

ACHIEVEMENT AND OUTPUT:

Alison's typing output is increasing as she gains in
experience. The use of a memory typewriter is a
tremendous help, eliminating re-types if work is changed
and enabling her to present typing of good quality.

USE OF SKILLS AND KNOWLEDGE:

Alison is quick to learn new tasks and tackles them with
enthusiasm.

INITIATIVE AND ORGANISING ABILITY:

The nature of Alison's work does not involve a great deal
of planning and organising ability as work is provided to
her when required.

TEAM WORKING AND ADAPTABILITY:

Alison is always willing to undertake any task asked of her
to the very best of her ability. She willingly helps out as
relief receptionist when required. A valuable team
member.

BUSINESS RELATIONS:

This is one of Alison's strongest points. She is an excellent
ambassador for the Bank, having a polite and helpful

telephone manner, giving a good 'first impression' of Regional Office.

OVERALL ASSESSMENT OF PERFORMANCE

Alison has now completed her first year with Barclays and during that time she has gained in confidence and experience. Despite, of course, certain restrictions, she tackles the work to the very best of her ability. She is a cheerful and friendly member of the secretarial team and we are very pleased to have her with us here at Regional Office.

M F Batt
Personnel Manager's Assistant
Date 22.5.89

**FUN AT REGIONAL OFFICE –
CHRISTMAS 1989**

"Have a good Christmas Al!!!"

said Alec - as I began my Christmas holiday.

"Thanks Alec - I certainly did!!! I was determined to have a Merry Christmas, followed by a very Happy New Year."

Christmas Eve for Larry and I, was spent getting slightly merry with our neighbours at 9 Coach House Court - Janie and Frank. I can't recall what Larry and Janie were drinking - but Frank was on the whisky, and I had a couple of snowballs. On leaving Janie and Frank's flat at a rather late hour - I think Frank had a pretty good idea about what Larry and I had in mind - my huge grin gave the game away!!

Our precious daughter, Emma Louise - was conceived in the early hours of Christmas Day morning - 1989.

Apprehension would be a good way to describe my thoughts and feelings on receiving a positive result from my second-time-round pregnancy test - I was absolutely delighted, but also very fearful of experiencing another miscarriage.

My mind was put at ease on Wednesday 18th April 1990 - at 3.15 p.m. as Larry and I attended my first scan appointment at the Rosie Maternity Hospital. To see Baby McGovern moving around inside me for the first time was an overwhelming experience - fantastic, to put it mildly! Larry and I didn't want to know the sex of our baby as we both thought it would be like opening an early Christmas present!! We were also

relieved to learn that I was only
expecting one baby, as opposed to
twins!!

*A full bladder is necessary for the success of this
examination. Drink a pint of water one hour before your
appointment and do not empty your bladder until the scan is
over. Your abdomen will be covered with gel during the scan –*
that was written on my scan appointment
letter.

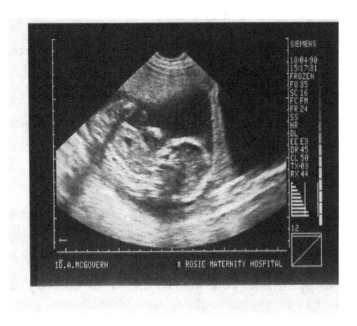

A MUCH TREASURED PICTURE

A full bladder is most definitely
what I had – in fact I had almost
reached bursting point, especially when
my tummy was prodded!! On completion of
my scan, I had to find the nearest
disabled loo as a matter of extreme
urgency!

Larry and I found the loos but, very
much to our surprise, there weren't any
for use by disabled people. "Wait
there, I'll go and get someone" – Larry
said. "No – if you leave me, I'll have
an accident – I'm desperate" – I

replied. So, between us, Larry and I managed to get me on to an ordinary loo - leaving my wheelchair outside the door. There weren't any grab-rails on the wall that I could use for support - only a wire-basket bin that I just about pulled off! Anyway, feeling absolutely exhausted, I finally managed to go to the loo - it was a huge relief, I can assure you!!

Being pregnant was thoroughly enjoyable - especially during the fourth to seventh month period. My morning sickness had thankfully passed. I didn't experience morning sickness though - more like evening sickness! I would quite often feel sick at around 6.30 p.m. One evening I really fancied a pizza - a huge mistake!! I soon found myself asking Larry for the bucket!! To feel my baby moving around inside me was an immeasurable experience. Baby McGovern's movements began as extremely gentle butterfly-like movements - then as my pregnancy progressed, soon developed into very prominent kicks!! Baby McGovern would also respond to music, as well as my voice - very very special moments.

My colleagues at Barclays were delighted for me. I didn't have to break my great news to Viv - she could tell by the sheer delight on my face! I will never ever forget the response received from a Manager called Peter Waggitt - a real comedian, to say the least!! "Pregnant - bloody hell, how the hell did you manage to do that?!!!!" "Just like anybody else thank you very much" - I replied!!!

TO ALL STAFF AT CAMBRIDGE REGIONAL OFFICE

2nd July 1990

As you all probably know I am temporarily retiring from work on Friday 6th July, to prepare for the long awaited arrival of Baby McGovern. He/She is due on or around 16th September!

I would very much like you to join Larry and I for a drink, (non alcoholic for me!) at the Rose & Crown, between 12-2 p.m.

I look forward to seeing you all.

ALISON McGOVERN

**VIV ALISON MARGARET JEAN
LYNN AND ALISON**

I was given a great send-off in the days leading up to my maternity leave. As well as a general get together at the Rose & Crown Pub in Histon, I was asked to join the two receptionists and some members of Cambridge Regional Office secretarial team, for a 'good luck' meal at the Travellers Rest – a Beefeater Restaurant, on Huntingdon Road in Cambridge.

**"GOOD LUCK ALISON" –
FRIDAY 6TH JULY 1990**

    With just six weeks to go before my
due date, I was now very pleased to not
have to think about going to work for a
while, as I had become, not only quite
large – but suddenly very tired.

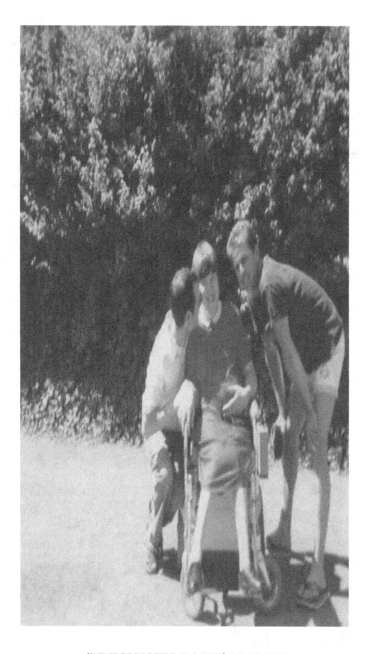

**'PREGNANT PROUD' ALISON
WITH LARRY AND PETE**

"You look like a beached whale Al"
said Pete, when he saw me resting on our
bed during a visit to Cambridge in
August 1990. "I have to say that I felt
extremely proud to be called a beached
whale Pete - thank you very much!!"

**PETE AND LISA ON THEIR WEDDING DAY
IN HATHERLEIGH DEVON –
SATURDAY 1ST SEPTEMBER 1990**

Despite not feeling too good on Pete and Lisa's special day – due to high blood pressure and blurred vision, Pete and Lisa were very much in my thoughts. At around the time that Pete and Lisa would have been saying their marriage vows to each other, there was also a hive of activity going on in the McGovern household. My midwife Carol was carrying out one of my many antenatal check-ups, and as a result of my present condition was debating on whether I should now be admitted to the Rosie.

Only two days later, on Monday 3rd September, Carol's question was answered. My blood pressure had reached such a high point – hospital was now the best place for me.

Personally, I was very relieved. I knew that I would now be receiving 24 hour care for both Baby McGovern and myself.

Over the next nine days my blood pressure remained quite stable. During the early hours of Wednesday, 12th September, I began experiencing Braxton Hicks (practice labour) contractions, but nothing came of them.

On the morning of Thursday 13th September, after a visit to the loo, the midwife looking after me at that moment suddenly began to get very excited. I had begun passing blood very slightly – a clear sign that I would soon be a Mum! Following an internal examination, it was discovered that despite Baby McGovern's head now being engaged within my pelvis, Baby McGovern was nowhere near ready to come into the world. He/She was very content to stay put!

Knowing that I was happy pressing on with my knitting, (an uncompleted blanket for Baby McGovern!) Larry thought he would grab the opportunity to return home for a couple of hours that afternoon. Within about thirty minutes of Larry's departure I began to feel desperately tired – possibly due to the fact that I had dropped no end of stitches!!

The next thing I knew I was lying on my bed feeling extremely ill. My head was pounding and my vision was severely blurred - I was also seeing strange dots in front of my eyes. I called out in desperation as a midwife was thankfully walking passed my side-room door. On catching her attention she immediately asked me what my symptoms were, and also took my blood pressure. Unknown to me at the time, I was suffering from pre-eclampsia - a condition in late pregnancy which, if not treated quickly, can be fatal for both the expectant mother and her unborn child.

"Larry will have my baby for me when he returns to my room and discovers that I have disappeared in my bed - he will be so worried" - I said to two midwifes as I was being wheeled in my bed, at approximately 4.30 p.m. to the Delivery Suite.

6.00 p.m. - still no sign of Larry! I later learnt that due to a set of traffic lights breaking down somewhere in the middle of Cambridge, Larry had got caught in a traffic jam during his return journey to the hospital.

Feeling so ill and fearing for my baby's health - I could sense that the medical staff were highly concerned for my health too. I was prepared for an emergency caesarean section, under general anaesthetic - at around 6.15 p.m. Very much to my relief, just as I was being taken through to the operating theatre, Larry and I were finally reunited - I was then given the opportunity to say an extremely tearful "goodbye" to him. I had now become very very frightened.

Obviously whilst asleep under general anaesthetic, I was totally unaware of all the activity that was now taking place within the operating theatre. At approximately 6.28 p.m. on Thursday 13th September 1990, our beautiful and much treasured, daughter, Emma Louise, entered this big wide world – weighing a nice healthy 7lb 9ozs. Larry was absolutely chuffed to be present at the birth of his brand new baby daughter.

From the second our Emma was born, Larry and I knew that she would be making television news! The story behind this is – in the final few days leading up to Emma's arrival, Larry and I were introduced to Stewart White – a news presenter from BBC Look East. Stewart and his camera crew were in the process of compiling a feature about Addenbrooke's Hospital and the Rosie – asked if Larry and I (and our Emma!) would like to be part of it. We were more than happy to oblige!!

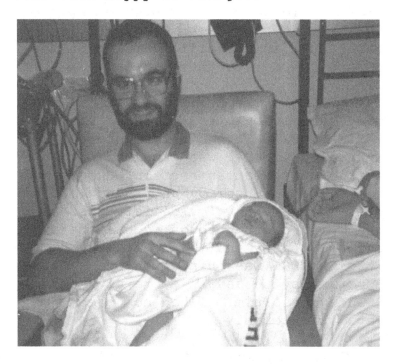

**A VERY PROUD MOMENT
FOR LARRY**

"You've got a baby girl Ali" - I heard Gaynor, the Midwifery Manager saying as I found myself gradually coming round from my general anaesthetic. "Thank god for that - my dream has come true" - I immediately thought.

BBC

S O U T H   &   E A S T

BRITISH BROADCASTING CORPORATION

ST CATHERINE'S CLOSE
ALL SAINTS GREEN
NORWICH
NORFOLK NR1 3ND
TELEPHONE: 0603 619331/2/3
TELEX: 97352
FAX: 0603 667865

24th October 1990

Mr & Mrs L McGovern
3, Coach House Court
Hawthorn Way
CAMBRIDGE
CB4 1BT

Dear Mr & Mrs McGovern

It was really wonderful to speak to you yesterday and find out that you
are all in good health and enjoying family life.

Please accept the enclosed video of the birth of your baby with our
compliments. I know you will enjoy watching it together.

Wishing you every happiness for the future.

Yours sincerely

L J Cooke
Newsroom Supervisor

CHAPTER
TEN

FAMILY LIFE

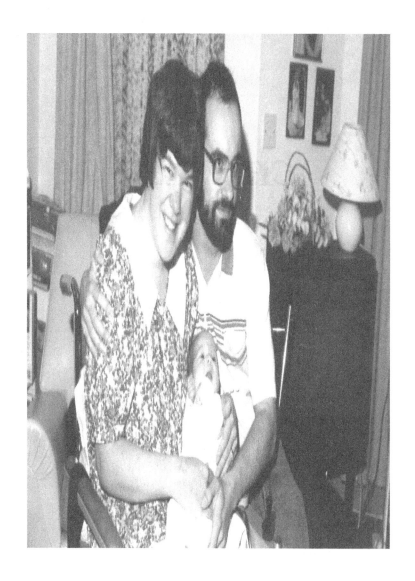

A FAMILY OF THREE

NEWBORN EMMA –
ABSOLUTE PRIDE AND JOY
FOR ALISON

BARCLAYS BANK PLC
Cambridge Regional Office
P.O. Box No. 90, Mortlock House, Histon, Cambridge CB4 4ZX
Telephone: (0223) 232133

Mr & Mrs L McGovern
3 Coach House Court
Hawthorn Way
CAMBRIDGE

Your Ref:
Our Ref: LG/KR
Ext: 3066

14 September 1990

Dear Larry & Alison

We are delighted to hear of the safe arrival of your new baby, Emma Louise.

All of us here at Regional Office send our warmest congratulations and best wishes to you and your family for your future health and happiness.

Yours sincerely

E P Gwynn

MRS LIZ GWYNN
RECRUITMENT OFFICER

Facsimile: (0223) 232159
Member of IMRO

Registered in London, England. Reg. No: 1026167. Reg. Office: 54 Lombard Street, London EC3P 3AH

BARCLAYS BANK PLC

Cambridge Regional Office

P.O. Box No. 90, Mortlock House, Histon, Cambridge CB4 4ZX

Telephone: (0223) 232133

Mrs A McGovern   Your Ref:
3 Coach House Court   Our Ref: JB/PAG
Hawthorn Way   Ext:
CAMBRIDGE

17 September 1990

Dear Alison

I was delighted to hear of the birth of your baby daughter, Emma, on the 13th September 1990. I am sure that both you and Larry are delighted with this news and I hope that you are recovering nicely.

I understand that the birth has made television news and perhaps you will let us know when this is likely to be shown. Please send us a photograph for the Bank Notes Magazine and I hope that you will pop in to see us when you are feeling better.

With kind regards.

J Baptie

MRS JULIE BAPTIE

Facsimile: (0223) 232159

Member of IMRO

Registered in London, England. Reg. No: 1026167. Reg. Office: 54 Lombard Street, London EC3P 3AH

A BIG YAWN FOR LITTLE EMMA!!!

I received plenty of visitors following the arrival of Emma - one who deserves a very special mention, is my brother Pete. Pete was so eager to meet his new niece. Within hours of Emma's birth, Pete drove all the way from Hatherleigh in Devon to Cambridge, on his motorbike. Spent an hour or two with Larry, Emma and I - before driving back again. "That meant an awful lot to me Pete - thank you so much."

There is no place like home. I felt like the proudest person in the world on the day that Larry and I took Emma home for the first time.

**ALISON WITH HER LITTLE GIRL –
FEELING EXTREMELY HAPPY**

**EMMA AGED 6 WEEKS –
WITH ALISON**

HANNANEWS

THE MAGAZINE FOR ALL WHO HAVE PASSED THROUGH
DAME HANNAH ROGERS SCHOOL

EDITOR: **JACK GATES**
EDITOR'S ASSISTANT: **JANE BRADFORD**
TEL: **KINGSBRIDGE (0548) 853979**

ST. GORAN
21, BELLE CROSS ROAD
KINGSBRIDGE,
DEVON.
TQ7 1NL

22ND, NOVEMBER, 1990

Dear Alison and Larry and Emma,

Thank you very much for your letter and especially the photo of Alison with Emma. Indeed, Emma is as lovely as her mother!

I think I might be able to reproduce it in Hannanews for all to see. It is unfortunate that we can't print in colour and sometimes the reproduction doesn't do justice to the subject, but we'll do our best.

Glad that Larry is coping with his new fatherhood responsibilities and I'm only sorry I got rid of my army gas-mask many years ago or I would have let him have it!

I hope Alison doesn't find it too hard getting back into the banking routine after her period of intensive motherhood.

If your Hannanews doesn't arrive before Christmas it will be Bill Evans's fault. I have everything ready for the printers and have been waiting over a week for his letter! I fear the printers won't have time to get it done in time now. It's very frustrating!

Thank you for your Christmas card. What a lovely picture. Hope you have a happy time. Will Emma hang up a stocking? It will only be a very small one!

Love to you all,

Jack
X

A Christmas card from Lynn Rawlings – another friend from Dame Hannah Rogers School read:-

When I got your lovely Christmas card,
I was so thrilled to see,
That you have got a baby girl,
Who's perfect as can be!
I had to write a poem,
To tell you that I'm proud,
'Cause I can't get up to Cambridge,
To say "well done" out loud!

XXXXXXXX for Baby Emma!

To Ali, Larry and Emma,

Have a fun-filled Christmas
and a new year to match!

Love,

Lynn.   xxxxxxxxxxxxxxxx

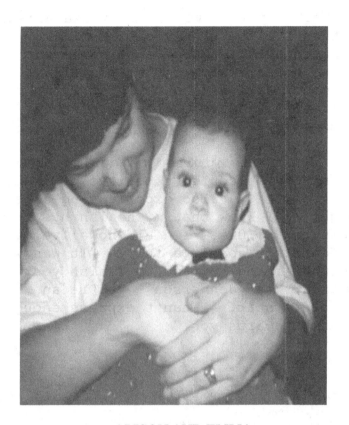

**ALISON AND EMMA –
MARCH 1991**

Returning to work following my maternity leave, on Wednesday 2nd January 1991, was unfortunately short-lived. On Tuesday 19th March, I was admitted to Hinchingbrooke Hospital in Huntingdon, for a hysterectomy. To be totally frank, I was extremely relieved, as my gynaecological health problems had now become so severe – I could no longer cope with them, and they were ruling my life.

"Don't worry love – all your problems will be over this time tomorrow" said Judy (the best nurse I have ever met) as she was helping to clean me up following an acute haemorrhage during the evening before my operation.

"I'll just have a cup of tea Alison
– then I'll be with you." My
gynaecologist – Miss Jennerson, said
those words, which sit very clearly in
my mind, as I lay on the trolley in the
operating theatre on the morning of
Wednesday, 20th March.

When Larry visited me during that
evening – he couldn't believe how well I
looked. I was also experiencing a real
high, as I knew that my health had been
restored – 100%. I could now live my
life to the absolute full. "It was well
worth waiting for you to finish your cup
of tea, Miss Jennerson – you're an
absolute star. I can't express enough
thanks towards you."

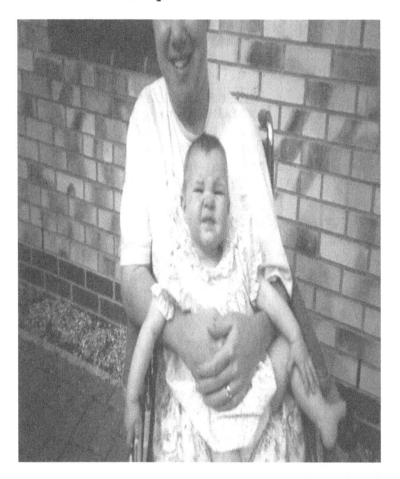

'FOOT DRIVER' EMMA!!!

From now on, my life just got better
and better - no more health problems -
fantastic! Larry, Emma and I could
really enjoy ourselves - we had a lot to
look forward to as a family.

A newspaper cutting read:-

Work to start on special home

WORK is to start on a special home for a disabled couple.

Housing Society Hundred Houses is set to begin conversion of a house at Fallowfield, Chesterton, on Monday for Larry and Alison McGovern, who have cerebral palsy.

The conversion, with wheelchair ramps and easy-to-reach facilities will take three months.

The couple and their year-old daughter Emma currently live in a two-room flat in Hawthorn Way, Cambridge.

PHOTO COURTESY OF CAMBRIDGE EVENING NEWS NEWSPAPER

A GREAT FAMILY PHOTO

**ALISON EMMA AND PETE –
FEBRUARY 1992**

**LITTLE EMMA IN HER NEW HOME –
APRIL 1992**

Larry, Emma and I moved into our new home in Fallowfield – in Chesterton, on Monday 6th April 1992. On being greeted with so much space, Larry and I both jokingly, felt the use of a map to find our way around would be very useful!!

Only a fortnight later, we had another special event to think about – Emma's christening at St. Andrew's Church, Chesterton – on Easter Sunday – 19th April.

**A SPECIAL MOMENT FOR EMMA
AND REVEREND JONATHAN SHELDON**

I thoroughly enjoyed Emma's special day – to think that our little girl was not only christened on Easter Sunday, but also at the same church where Larry and I married – that carries a huge amount of sentimental value in my opinion – wonderful!

A big fat zero – that was what I was able to type in the *'NO. OF DAYS SICKNESS ABSENCE DURING THE LAST 12 MONTHS'* box on my Performance Appraisal form – at work, for the year ending May 1992. The comments read:-

ACHIEVEMENT AND OUTPUT:

Alison's Secretarial output is of a good standard and her work is methodical. She assists with Reception duties on a relief basis and deals with incoming calls as quickly as possible.

USE OF SKILLS AND KNOWLEDGE:

Alison has improved her knowledge of the Xerox typewriter over the past 12 months.

INITIATIVE AND ORGANISING ABILITY:

Alison's role does not involve a great deal of planning.

TEAM WORKING AND ADAPTABILITY:

A willing and helpful member of the Section. Alison will attempt any task to the very best of her ability.

CUSTOMER SERVICE:

Alison's telephone answering continues to be of a very high standard. She is friendly and always polite when dealing with visitors at Regional Office and numerous compliments have been made.

OVERALL ASSESSMENT OF PERFORMANCE

Alison has produced a good years work. She continues to undertake typing work for the Advances Section, but has also been recently introduced to work emanating from CWIP and Administration Sections. Her knowledge of the Xerox typewriter has improved over the past 12 months and she now understands more fully the various functions.

She is proving to be a reliable team member.

C A Jackson
Assistant Personnel Manager

Date 1st May 1992

Roy Webber - the Personnel Manager,
later gave me a copy of his letter:-

Barclays Group Staff Union

BARCLAYS BANK PLC
JUXON HOUSE
94 ST. PAUL'S CHURCHYARD
LONDON EC4M 8EH

TEL. 01-248 9155
EXT. 3375, 3378, 3376, 3188, 3359, 3195

May 1992

Dear Roy,

Now that I have retired I have a little time to write to you to
express my thanks for the kind and considerate way that you
and your colleagues at Cambridge treated me on my visits.

It was always a pleasure to travel to Cambridge, a lovely city,
and know that whatever the case involved it would be dealt with
on a practical and sympathetic basis.

My thanks to you Roy in particular, but please also pass on my
thanks to Tony Mott, Colin Johnson, Graham Mickley and
especially Alison who always made me smile with her positive
attitude towards her disability.

Best wishes,

Dennis

B.G.S.U.: A Certificated Independent Trade Union

Get Well Soon

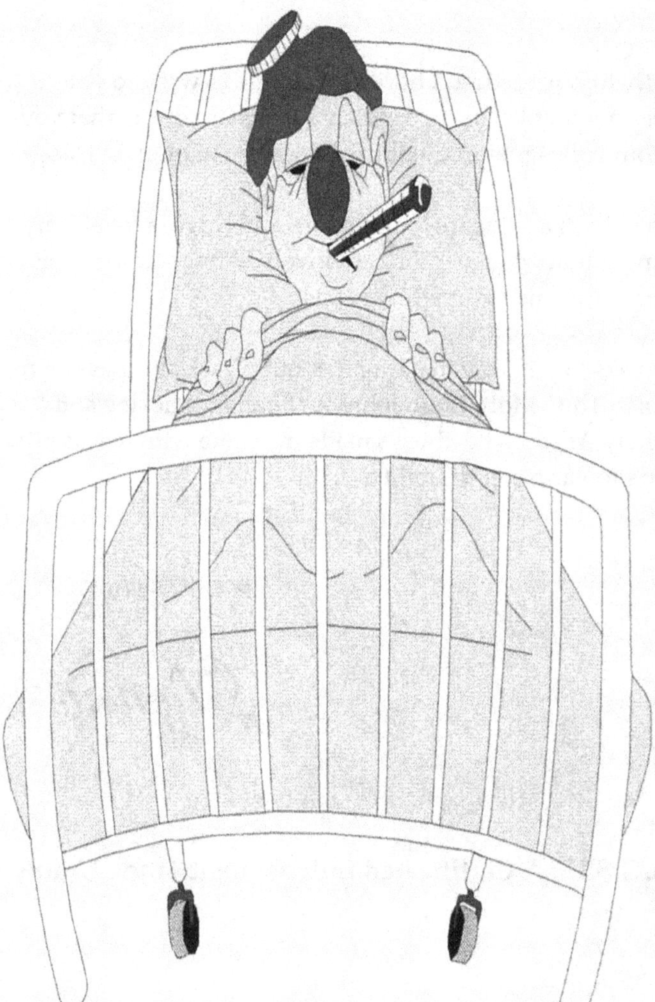

CHAPTER ELEVEN

NEAR DISASTER STRIKES

ALL IS WELL
THAT ENDS WELL

**PICTURE COURTESY OF THE BIG SHEEP
BIDEFORD DEVON**

*"Didn't we have a luver'ly day
the day we went to The Big Sheep!!"*

Yes – Larry, Emma and I had a great family day out with Mum and Dad, at The Big Sheep – near Bideford in Devon, on Saturday 17th April 1993. There was plenty to see and do – including:-

Sheep Milking
Sheep Shearing
Duck Trialling
Baby Lambs
A Woodcraft Centre
Sheep Dog Trials
The 'Sheepy Shop' and Restaurant

ALISON WITH TWO BIG SHEEP!!

221

The highlight of my day at The Big Sheep was becoming the owner of a racing sheep for the day, and having a flutter! I haven't got a clue what my adopted sheep was called – or what position he or she ended the race at, but all the same, it gave me a great laugh – I would most certainly spend another day at The Big Sheep!!!

**LARRY AND MUM
WITH EMMA – OUR LITTLE LAMB!!**

As well as spending time in Devon that weekend – Mum, Dad, Larry, Emma and I spent time in Cornwall with Gran and Grandpa. Pete and Lisa also joined us. My times with Gran and Grandpa were always very enjoyable.

**FOUR GENERATIONS –
GRAN ANDREWS ALISON MUM AND EMMA**

EMMA WITH –
DAD LARRY GRANDPA ANDREWS AND PETE

Inevitably, after having such a good time with my family down in the West Country – I soon found myself, not only back at home in East Anglia, but sitting at my desk at work in Histon.

On Wednesday 12th May, I awoke feeling not too good – but me being me, still attended work despite having flu-like symptoms – aching limbs, feeling cold one minute and very hot the next, and a headache. I felt that I had taken more than my fair share of time off work, so decided to battle on.

Waking up on Thursday 13th May, I immediately thought, "I don't think I'm going to manage a full day at work today, but I'm determined to give it a go." Dosing myself up with paracetamol, I then asked Larry to drive me to the office (with Emma) as usual.

Whilst doing some typing for Nigel Routley, (sorry Nigel – please don't

take this personally!!) I remember
thinking that Icouldn't press another
key on my keyboard - I was now in
desperate need of my bed.

"Happy Birthday for tomorrow Val" I
said to Val Clements as she was walking
up the office staircase - while I was
waiting for Larry to collect me.

I got into bed at around lunchtime
on that Thursday afternoon - and that
was where I stayed for the whole
weekend, apart from getting up to go to
the loo occasionally.

My 27th birthday - Monday 17th May,
was spent as an inpatient at
Addenbrooke's Hospital - in a bed on the
gynaecology ward - there were no other
beds available. My health had
deteriorated so much over that past
weekend. Dr. Robson - my GP decided to
call an ambulance and admit me to
hospital for tests - mainly to rule out
the possibility of meningitis.

One of those tests was a lumbar
puncture. This involved removing a
sample of fluid through a needle from
the space surrounding my spinal cord.
Putting it mildly, it was absolute agony
for me, but having such an
understanding, caring and patient doctor
carrying out the procedure - helped me
through it. Apparently my lower back
was black and blue afterwards - and I
felt as though I'd been run over by a
bus!

The doctors in charge of my care
were subsequently satisfied that I
wasn't suffering from meningitis - and
assured that I was feeling a lot better
in myself, allowed me to return home on
18th May.

"I'm going to have to go now - I'm not feeling very well" - I said to Frank, after receiving a phone call from him wishing me a happy belated birthday during that evening. I suddenly felt very very hot. Just as I'd placed the telephone receiver back on its base - I received a really weird sensation in my head.

With the benefit of hindsight, I had suffered a brain aneurism - better known as a brain haemorrhage. This is a sudden leak of blood, and is caused by the rupture of a weakened blood vessel. Personally, the sensation that I felt in my head, (I'll never ever forget it) was similar to biting into a liquor chocolate and the alcohol immediately spills out into your mouth.

The events from now on are very erratic. I can remember pushing myself towards our bedroom door and on the way saying to Larry, "Get somebody quick" - I wasn't able to elaborate any further due to the pain in my head being so acute.

Ibuprofen - a drug given to me by Dr. Hughes didn't help my situation at all. As the night progressed I knew that I was in serious trouble. Our bed was soaking wet as a result of my temperature being dangerously high. "Larry - I need a doctor now." Within seconds of me saying that to Larry - the slightest movement of my body would make me vomit profusely.

The journey by ambulance back to Addenbrooke's in the early hours of Wednesday 19th May, was extremely slow. I also couldn't stop apologising to the two ambulance men for making such a mess in the ambulance!!

Finding myself alone in a dark room before being transferred to a side-room on Ward G5 was the next thing that I was aware of. "She's had a brain haemorrhage," I heard someone say. A CT scan had apparently established that a few minutes earlier.

The majority of my treatment was done through drug therapy and almost constant observation.

On arriving in the side-room, I had no choice but to lay in my bed, in total darkness. I could not bear to see even the least possible amount of light at that stage.

Now, and for the next eleven days I was bed-bound - lying permanently on my back - but thankfully was able to cope with seeing light again. I wasn't able to do anything for myself. I was totally reliant on the medical staff for feeding, toileting etc., etc. Larry was an absolute gem in providing me with as much help as he possibly could - I will always be more than grateful to him for that.

On Sunday 30th May a nurse called Tracey said that I was allowed to get out of bed. This information was wrong and through getting out of bed too early - on Monday 31st May, I suffered a relapse. Severe headaches and vomiting had returned with vengeance. Deep depression had also set in - I honestly thought that I was now going to die.

"If there is a God - please, I desperately need your help now. Larry and I have only been married a few years, but more importantly, I can't bear the thought of our Emma growing up without her Mum - she is only 2½ years old. I have also got far too much to do." That was what came into my mind as I once again began several days of being totally bed-bound.

Worse was yet to come. On Wednesday 2nd June, whilst on a bedpan, I suddenly started to feel myself rising towards the ceiling - extremely scary. Again, with the benefit of hindsight, I later learnt that I had had two grand-mal epileptic fits, (the first in my life) - one of which, very nearly took my life.

"Thank Christ for that - I'm still alive" - I thought to myself as I regained consciousness. "My headache has greatly reduced. I can't see though - I've gone blind." My speech was affected due to biting my tongue. I had also been transferred to a high dependency unit within Addenbrooke's. A high dependency unit is an area for patients who require more intensive observation, treatment and nursing care than is usually provided on a general ward. It is a standard of care between the general ward and full intensive care.

Now that I could cope with the degree of pain in my head - I was determined to fight my illness - it was not going to ruin the life that I had been given. During the next ward-round I talked to my doctors about my concerns relating to my sight. Thankfully this problem was short-lived, and was due to blood pressing on the optic nerve - as well as bruising.

I was overwhelmed by the amount of letters and get well cards/messages, flowers and visitors that I received during those long weeks in hospital. **"Thank you so much everybody - your**

love, best wishes, help, support and
prayers contributed greatly to me making
a full recovery."

TELEPHONE HISTON (0220) 232133   Mortlock House
                                        P O Box 90
                                        Histon
                                        Cambridge
                                        CB4 4ZX

                    May 25th 1993

Dear Larry,

I have just returned to work after a week's holiday; and was so sorry to hear about
Alison's illness. This is just to send you and her best wishes from all of us here for a
quick recovery. We are all thinking a lot about the three of you. I know that you will
let us know if there is any way in which we may be able to help.

                                Yours sincerely

                                Harry Faure Walker

                                11, Saltrens Cottages,
                                Monkleigh,
                                Bideford EX39 5JP

                                2.6.93.

Dear Ali,

        I've just been talking to a very nice staff nurse, who says
that you haven't had such a good day today, and that you're
waiting to go for another scan. Of course, by the time you get
this letter, we'll all know a bit more, and hopefully, you'll be
feeling much better.

        I've enclosed these photos, taken when you were all down
with us. Little did we know what was around the corner. You
have been such a fighter all your life, that I'm sure you'll come
through this with your determination and pluck.

        Dad went back to sea today, for the usual 3 weeks tour,
let's hope you're home by the time he's home again.

        We had a lovely time with Emma, she has inherited your
gentle nature, but not your appetite! She brought us a lot of

pleasure and happiness, and we think that she enjoyed herself too. We've taken more photos of course, and Dad has the camera on board now, so we'll have to wait for those snaps. She used to come into our bedroom each morning to look out of the window for the sheep and listen to the birds.

Do you remember how you used to collect wild flowers Ali? Well, your daughter likes to pick buttercups and daisies. She liked the beach too, and collected some shells, and she washed all the sand off in the bird bath – she doesn't mind the birds having a bath, but she didn't like it at all!

How is Larry coping with everything? We would have liked to have been able to help for much longer. I expect Emma has been to play school today and Larry has been able to stay with you.

Pete and Lisa move house soon, they'll be happy about that. Then Seamus their cat can come out of the cattery and Levi can have a good run in the back yard. Dad is going to build her a kennel.

We are all looking forward to seeing Julia when she comes and she's looking forward to seeing us too.

I went back to work today and everyone is asking after you and hope you'll be well again soon.

Hope you like the photos and that they cheer you up a bit.

I must get ready for bed now – up early again in the morning.

You hurry up and get better now Ali, we are always thinking about you. Dad rang Nana when we got home and she says that she is going to write to you.

All for now.

Lots of love from
Mum   x x x

Sunday afternoon

6/6/93

Dear Alison,

I'm sorry to hear you are not well in hospital.

I would like you to know that we are all thinking of you and that you were remembered in our prayers with Larry and Emma as well in this morning's service.

So please get well soon. We all miss you, it seems a long time since I last saw you all. I wish you all the very best and hope your health will improve soon.

Lots of love to you
        from
                Margaret (SMITH)

    The first major milestone towards my full recovery happened on Monday, 21st June 1993 – a highly emotional, but very special day. Yes – I had made such good progress that I was discharged from hospital. The image of several nurses waving goodbye to me (a couple in tears) at the window of Ward G5 will remain with me for a long time to come. I was also having problems holding back the tears!!

    To know that I was at home with Larry and Emma again was, without a doubt – fantastic. The same applied to Julia's visit during that summer.

ALISON
BACK HOME WITH LARRY AND EMMA
(JULY 1993)

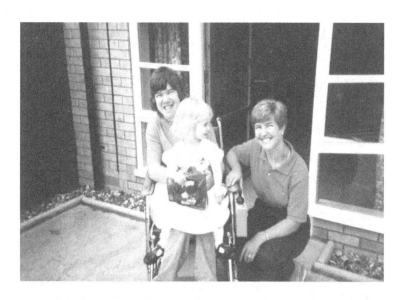

JULIA EMMA AND ALISON

**EMMA BY THE RIVER CAM –
WAITING TO FEED THE DUCKS**

Before satisfying my second major milestone - returning to work, I was required to return to hospital for a second angiogram. My stay thankfully, was only 24 hours!!

An angiogram is an x-ray examination that enabled the radiologist to study the blood vessels in my brain. To begin with, a small hole in my groin area had to be made so that a catheter carrying a special dye could be inserted. Eager to get the whole procedure underway, I gave the doctor permission to use his scalpel. I immediately regretted that, as I hadn't allowed enough time for the local anaesthetic to work!!

I returned to my job at Barclays on Monday 11th October - straight away on a full-time basis. Obviously it was great to see all my friends again - and know that my life was now to a large degree, back to normal.

My Performance Appraisal Report - for the year ending 23rd May 1994 read:-

ACHIEVEMENT AND OUTPUT:

Although a very disrupted year due to serious illness her output continues to be of a good standard. The new Word For Windows has helped to improve her accuracy and Alison completed work at a speed commensurate with her capabilities.

USE OF SKILLS AND KNOWLEDGE:

She has responded well to the training on the new processor and has coped very well in learning the basic operation of the equipment. She will be able to build upon this and gain more experience over the coming months.

INITIATIVE AND ORGANISING ABILITY:

Alison shows adequate initiative to cope with the demands of her job and she is now being encouraged to collect and deliver work which gives her a greater sense of independence and achievement. Her new wheelchair has made quite a difference.

TEAM WORKING AND ADAPTABILITY:

She enjoys the company of her colleagues and is a cheerful member of the team. There is no task given to her that she will not attempt or give of her best.

CUSTOMER SERVICE AND MARKETING/SELLING SKILLS:

Always creates a favourable impression when undertaking relief reception duties. Polite and helpful to her colleagues and visitors to Regional Office.

OVERALL ASSESSMENT OF PERFORMANCE

Alison was off work for nearly five months due to a serious illness and we were all delighted that she made a full recovery and returned to work stronger and more determined than before to give a good service. Alison also had the challenge of new equipment and it is great credit to her that she has proved that very few tasks are beyond her. She has been encouraged to become more independent and has made very good progress on last year's performance – albeit she was only able to complete approximately 7 months work in the year. We are aware that Alison is not too keen on reception duties but her time on reception has been reduced as she now only covers for lunch/coffee breaks or occasional absence. As she is not able to undertake filing etc duties it does at least give her some variety otherwise she would be typing all day.

S R Hobbs
Senior Operations Manager

16 May 1994

REVIEWER'S COMMENTS

We were all delighted to see Alison return to work following her illness and to see that she has made a full recovery. She is a very popular and helpful member of the Regional Office Team and thoroughly deserves this good report.

R Webber

Personnel Manager   23.5.94

27th June, 1994

Hosp. No. 83 66 96

Mrs. Alison McGovern
73 Fallowfield
Cambridge.

Dear Mrs. McGovern,

I write with reference to your recent attendance at the Medical Out-patient Clinic at Addenbrooke's Hospital.

I am glad to say that I do not think that your history of subdural haemorrhage with normal angiography or presumed epilepsy is a contraindication to air travel. I would, therefore, be happy on medical grounds for you to proceed with arrangements for your holiday to America. I do think, however, that your recent "fits" may be better controlled on a different drug. I have written to your doctor with the recommendations and would be grateful if you could get in touch with her over the next few days to discuss your future therapy.

I trust that you remain well and very much hope that you have a rewarding holiday in America.

With kind regards.

Yours sincerely,

Dr. Brian Thomson
Hon. Senior Registrar to Dr. Rubenstein/Professor Sissons

BT/NJD.30.6.94.

Addenbrooke's NHS Trust
Hills Road, Cambridge CB2 2QQ
Telephone: (0223) 245151   Cambridge University Teaching Hospitals Trust

"Thank you Dr. Thomson - I had an absolutely fantastic time in Florida with Larry and Emma." Our two week holiday in May 1996 took two years to plan!! We had three main reasons for

235

jetting off to America – to attend
Julia's graduation ceremony, to take
Emma to Disney World, and celebrate
Julia's and my 30th birthday together.

    Before embarking on our 8 hour and
40 minute flight to Orlando on Thursday
2nd May, courtesy of Virgin Atlantic –
Larry, Emma and I decided to spoil
ourselves by spending the previous night
at the London Hilton Hotel – Gatwick.

JET-SET EMMA!!

Our reunion with Julia and Chip was
fabulous - again, I had problems holding
back the tears!! We all then had a 2½
hour drive to Julia and Chip's house in
Jacksonville. Whilst travelling on the
highway, I kept saying to myself, "Yes,
I am in America!!"

GRADUATION DAY FOR JULIA

To witness Julia receiving her
degree in Journalism at the University
of Florida - which she'd spent the past
seven years studying for, was a highly
emotional experience for me - I felt
like the proudest person in the world
that day. The atmosphere was absolutely
wonderful - I have never experienced
anything like it in my life.

1,800 graduates, all individually
received their degrees in various
subjects - 900 in the morning, and a
further 900 in the afternoon. Larry,
Emma and I attended the afternoon
session - that took 3 hours to
complete!! No, we were certainly not
bored - Emma was contented with her
colouring book and crayons.

**A MOMENTOUS OCCASION –
4TH MAY 1996**

Sunday, 5th May was a day of rest
and recuperation – either beside, or in
Julia and Chip's pool – in their back
garden.

"SAFETY CONSCIOUS EMMA!!!"

**"CHEERS EVERYONE -
IT'S ONLY WATER!!!"**

During the following day - Julia,
Larry, Emma and I headed towards Disney
World. Chip's Mum, Carol also joined
us. Emma was in her element - she would
soon be meeting Mickey Mouse and all his
friends.

So that we could appreciate the
Disney World experience - prior to our
visit, Julia booked us all into a hotel
called All-Star Music. Due to Disney
World being so huge - 40 square miles in
total, we decided to focus on the Magic
Kingdom Theme Park for the majority of
our two day stay.

**A 'MAGIC KINGDOM'
FOR EMMA ALISON AND LARRY**

I began our fun-packed day on
Tuesday 7th May by eating (not all!!!)
of an extremely gooey cake! I was so
amazed by it – I kept thinking, "Surely,
this isn't what is eaten for
breakfast?!!!"

"BREAKFAST IN AMERICA!!!"

"Where's Mickey – where's Mickey?"
Emma kept saying. Her little face lit
up like a torch when she finally found
him!!

**A VERY SPECIAL MOMENT
FOR EMMA**

EMMA MEETS MINNIE TOO

AND DONALD DUCK!!
(FOLLOWED BY)

FUN IN A TEACUP!!!

**LARRY AND ALISON
ON MAIN STREET USA!!!**

At three o'clock that afternoon,
Emma, Larry, Julia, Carol and I watched
the daily parade. Then in the evening
we arranged for us all to have dinner
with the Disney characters - which, I
have to say, was thoroughly enjoyable -
Emma ate not a lot of dinner!!!

FUN WITH PLUTO!!

A HUG WITH GOOFY!!!

Ahead of leaving Orlando altogether, Chip was able to join in with all the fun during a trip to Sea World. I was most impressed by Shamu and his family - very very entertaining.

ACROBATIC SHAMU

The events surrounding the big '*30*' for Julia and I, included a lot more swimming in Julia and Chip's pool, far too much sunbathing on my part - Julia will no doubt agree with that!!!! Retail therapy, a trip to the zoo where I refused to go anywhere near the Reptile House - and finally, I was none-the-wiser after attending an American Baseball match!!

"Happy Birthday To You, Happy Birthday To You, Happy Birthday Dear Alison and Julia, Happy Birthday To You."

It was just great to spend our 30th birthday together - the perfect end to a very memorable holiday.

"HAPPY" BIRTHDAY GIRLS!!

Saying goodbye to Julia and Chip at Orlando International Airport was, as always, immensely difficult for me - I was an emotional wreck. Desperate not to lose sight of my twin sister, in particular.

"HOME IS WHERE THE HEART IS"
SAY PONGO AND TIGER!!!

Virgin Atlantic Airways l
Sussex House
High Street
Crawley
West Sussex RH10 1BZ
Customer Relations: 0129
Baggage Claims: 01293 4·
fax: 01293 747750

Ref : JS/074628/2/MCG

19 July 1996

Mrs A Mcgovern
73 Fallowfield
Chesterton
Cambridge
CB4 1PE

Dear Mrs Mcgovern,

Thank you so much for your recent letter to Richard Branson. Richard has
asked that I reply on his behalf and sends his heartfelt thanks for your
letter.

We were delighted that you enjoyed your recent flight with Virgin
Atlantic to Orlando and you may be assured that your kind remarks have
been passed to the relevant Departments and Managers.

We have enclosed details of our frequent flyer scheme for your perusal.
Once again Mrs McGovern, thank you so much for taking the time to write
to us with your kind words and we look forward to welcoming you on board
one of our flights again soon.

Yours sincerely

Cheryl Porter (Miss)
Customer Relations Executive

Registered Office: 120 Campden Hill Road, London W8 7AR. Registered in England 1600117. VAT Number: GB425·2161·84

Only three months later – during late August 1996, I was also faced with having to say goodbye to Pete and Lisa. They were about to begin their new life together in New Zealand. It goes without saying – that too was a highly emotional occasion.

EAST ANGLIAN NEUROSURGERY & HEAD INJURY SERVICE

Mr R Macfarlane

Tel 01223 217289

Box no 166

25 November 1996

836696/55993

Mrs Alison McGovern
73 Fallowfield
Cambridge
CB4 1PE

Addenbrooke's NHS Trust
Hills Road
Cambridge CB2 2QQ

Dear Mrs McGovern

Following a request from Dr Rubenstein I had arranged to see you as an Out Patient on the 11th February, However, I have received a letter from Dr Bastable to say that you have already decided to discontinue your anticonvulsants. Under the circumstances, I have cancelled that appointment, but will be pleased to see you if there are any problems.

Yours sincerely

Robert Macfarlane MD FRCS
Consultant Neurosurgeon

Copy to

Copy to

Dr R Bastable
Nuffield Road Medical Centre
Nuffield Road
Cambridge
CB4 1GL

Dr D Rubenstein
Consultant Physician
Addenbrooke's Hospital NHS Trust
(box no 153)

```
        I ended the year of 1996 satisfying
myself by achieving my third, and final,
milestone towards a full recovery
following my brain haemorrhage.
Medication for epilepsy was no longer
required.  My long fight may have taken
2½ years to complete, but I could now
look forward to living a healthy life
once more.  What more can I ask for?
Absolutely fantastic!
```

73 Fallowfield
Chesterton
Cambridge CB4 1PE

Telephone 01223 425093

4th December 1996

Dear Dr. Rubenstein,

I am writing to let you know that I have almost finished taking my medication for epilepsy and I am delighted to be able to inform you that I am feeling very very much better. I shall be returning to work on Monday.

May I take this opportunity to send my heartfelt thanks to you for all your help as it is greatly appreciated. It is absolutely wonderful to be feeling so well again. Please could you also pass on my thanks to Dr. Macfarlane. Thank you very much indeed.

With my very best wishes,

Alison McGovern

MRS ALISON McGOVERN

THANK YOU

CHAPTER TWELVE

1997 – NOT A YEAR TO BE REMEMBERED

FEBRUARY
AUGUST
OCTOBER

A BOUT OF
UNHAPPINESS

The day was Thursday, 6th February 1997 – my life was suddenly put into a state of utter mayhem. Coming to terms with the fact that my twin sister – to whom I am very close, was now living with, and undergoing treatment for breast cancer.

My immediate reaction on receiving such devastating news was to shed a huge of amount of tears, and drink a glass of white wine – maybe even two, at a rather brisk pace!!

For many weeks following the initial shock, I found that I was able to cope with my usual way of life one minute, and not the next. I felt a world away from Julia.

One day whilst sitting in the staff room, during my lunch hour – with tear-after-tear rolling down my face, my mind began to work overtime – as it quite often does!! With Julia not only ill, but also far away, I was longing to find a way of somehow being close to her. The Internet Provider – America Online (better known as AOL) came to my rescue, and since making that vital connection – I haven't looked back!

"If Julia is as positive as you are Alison – she'll be absolutely fine." Those words – said by my colleague and friend Alison Ayres, helped in a big way, to put my emotions back on an even keel at last. "Thanks Alison!!"

"Princess Diana is dead." That was my next blow – on Sunday 31st August. The outpouring of grief displayed by the British nation during those days leading up to Diana's funeral on Saturday, 6th September was out of the ordinary – a unique experience for a unique lady.

Personally, I kept recalling that occasion when Princess Diana said that single word to me, "Hello."

They say that things happen in three's. Sadly, on Thursday 9th October, our dear Candy passed away. I cried buckets of tears on that day too, but managed to avoid hitting the bottle!!

Candy may have only been a cat, but she was most definitely a cat – little at that, with a massive personality!! Larry originally collected her from a Wood Green Animal Shelter near Godmanchester, Cambridgeshire – in February 1987.

When I first moved to East Anglia to be with Larry, Candy was most put out because I had pinched her master – thankfully she soon came round!!

There is one particular occasion on which I remember Candy with great affection. When she followed Larry and I to church!! It was a service during which our banns were being read – to be totally honest, I was more concerned about Candy than anything else. Who was waiting for us outside the church door after the service? Yes, you've guessed it – Candy!!! How she managed to negotiate an extremely busy roundabout situated just outside Chesterton, is still beyond me – Candy must have been blessed with more than nine lives!!!

"IT'S MY WHEELCHAIR TOO"
SAYS CANDY!!!

CHAPTER THIRTEEN

A PROMISE MADE –
A PROMISE KEPT

NEW ZEALAND
SUNDAY 5TH AUGUST –
MONDAY 27TH AUGUST 2001

With 1997 being such a turbulent
year emotionally, I was now determined
to put a very unhappy period in my life
behind me, and move on.

In early 1998, after reaching a
compromise with my colleagues at
Barclays - which involved having a
purpose-built reception desk made to
suit my personal needs, I began my new,
extremely enjoyable role as Regional
Office Receptionist. I was now in my
element - total independence, the
opportunity to provide a high standard
of customer service - whilst still
maintaining my secretarial skills.

"I've got some big news for you!!"
Those were some of the words in a
message left on our answer-machine,
towards the beginning of July, spoken by
Julia. My twin sister was now starting
her new life back in England. From a
selfish point of view, I was absolutely
delighted to welcome Julia home. Sadly
Julia's marriage later ended in divorce.

20th May 1999, was, without a doubt
not one of my best days working for
Barclays. A fax was sent to all members
of staff within Regional Office. Sadly
that fax contained information which
inevitably meant redundancy - over a two
year period, for many of my colleagues
within Regional Office. Saying goodbye
to one hundred and thirty of my friends
- who I'd worked with for years,
obviously had an adverse affect on me.
I knew that my turn would eventually
come too - it was now just a case of
when.

My way of coping with the
uncertainty was to give myself something
nice to look forward to. I had always
been strong-minded about returning to

New Zealand in order to fulfil my long-term promise to my dear Nana. I thought now was a good chance to turn my dream into reality - otherwise it may be too late.

On Saturday, 7th October 2000, I really felt like getting out of my electric wheelchair and jumping up and down in front of everybody in the Travel Agents - I had just paid a £224.06 deposit, and booked a return flight from London Heathrow to Auckland International Airport - with my Emma accompanying me, on Sunday, 5th August 2001. I could have also kissed Austin - the clerk who actually accepted my booking!! "YIPPEE - I'm almost there!!!"

TRAVEL CHOICE

Travel Choice
6 Fitzroy Street
CAMBRIDGE
CB1 1EW

01223 464219

07-OCT-2000

Mrs A McGovern
73 Fallowfield
CAMBRIDGE
CB4 1PE

Dear Mrs McGovern

OUR REF:- 128-003288 05/08/2001

Thank you for choosing Travel Choice to book your recent holiday and we are pleased to enclose your confirmation documents for this forthcoming holiday on 05/08/2001 with Unijet Scheduled Flights.

We would ask you to check that the booking has been made according to your instructions. If you do have any queries about your booking please contact us immediately so that we can offer you our full assistance.

The outstanding balance of £1,675.00 is due on 27/05/2001 and we would be grateful if you could arrange for prompt payment in order that the administration of your booking proceeds smoothly. Please note that this amount may include the balance of any low deposit settled on your behalf and we would ask you to pay this amount by the agreed date. You may come into the shop to settle your account, or phone us if it is more convenient.

May we take this opportunity to remind you that we can supply foreign currency and travellers cheques at excellent rates. We can also organise any car hire, airport parking and many other additional services to make your holiday plans run as smoothly as possible.

Yours sincerely

Travel Choice

The date was Saturday, 28th April 2001 - I was longing to settle my account with Travel Choice. I have never been so happy to part with such a large amount of money!! My New Zealand dollars were ordered through Tesco, and delivered directly to me at home!

Unijet

ITINERARY

MCGOVERN A MRS
MCGOVERN E MISS

ITINERARY NO: 62549   DATE OF ISSUE: 19 JUL 2001   BOOKING REF: LG5L4C

SUNDAY 05 AUG 01		CONFIRMED
SINGAPORE AIRLINES	NON-STOP	FLIGHT: SQ 321
		CLASS: ECONOMY
DEPART:	LONDON HEATHROW:	22.15 HRS
ARRIVE:	SINGAPORE:	18.00 HRS 06 AUG
MEALS SERVED MEAL		

259

MONDAY 06 AUG 01 SINGAPORE AIRLINES	NON-STOP	CONFIRMED FLIGHT: SQ 285 CLASS: ECONOMY
DEPART: ARRIVE: MEALS SERVED MEAL	SINGAPORE: AUCKLAND:	20.45 HRS 10.05 HRS 07 AUG

SUNDAY 26 AUG 01 SINGAPORE AIRLINES	NON-STOP	CONFIRMED FLIGHT: SQ 286 CLASS: ECONOMY
DEPART: ARRIVE: MEALS SERVED MEAL	AUCKLAND: SINGAPORE:	14.15 HRS 20.45 HRS

SUNDAY 26 AUG 01 SINGAPORE AIRLINES	NON-STOP	CONFIRMED FLIGHT: SQ 322 CLASS: ECONOMY
DEPART: ARRIVE: MEALS SERVED MEAL	SINGAPORE LONDON HEATHROW	23.20 HRS 05.50 HRS 27 AUG

UNIJET WISH TO ADVISE YOU OF THE FOLLOWING:-

ALL SCHEDULE SERVICE PASSENGERS SHOULD RECONFIRM THEIR RETURN FLIGHT AT LEAST 72 HOURS BEFORE DEPARTURE. TELEPHONE NUMBERS CAN BE FOUND IN LOCAL DIRECTORIES.

At last the calendar read Sunday, 5th August 2001 - today was the day that Emma and I were off on our **big** trip to the other side of the world. Believe it or not, I was very very excited - I think Emma was too!!!

Once Emma and I had checked-in at Terminal 3 within London Heathrow Airport, and said our goodbyes to Larry - as well as our fairly sizeable suitcase, hold-all-bag and my walking frame, I knew that my adventure with our 10 year old daughter, was now, well and truly, happening - excellent!!!

The level of customer service provided - from checking-in at London Heathrow through to when Emma and I were met by Pete and Lisa, and their three children, Caitlin, and twins - James and Olivia, at Auckland International Airport could not be

faulted – Emma and I were extremely
well looked after. The hot spicy Asian
food given to us on the plane wasn't
very impressive though!!

The flight to Singapore took 12
hours – I must have slept for most of
that time because we seemed to arrive
there pretty quickly. Emma and I then
changed planes in Singapore – which
also included a two hour look around
the airport.

On boarding the plane to begin the
final leg of the journey from Singapore
to Auckland, I suddenly became
overwhelmed with immense excitement –
due to being surrounded by the New
Zealand accent in a big way!!! It was
at this precise moment that the reality
of my holiday dawned on me. In ten
hours time, Emma and I would be landing
in Auckland. It may have taken 13
years to achieve, but my Nana would now
be seeing me back in New Zealand. She
would be meeting her great grand
daughter for the first time too.

As a result of drinking plenty of
water to prevent dehydration, I needed
to pay several visits to the loo. Being
about an hour from landing in Auckland,
I asked for assistance again. The
toilet cubicle on an aircraft is at the
best of times, difficult to move around
in due to the extremely limited space.
Managing to close the concertina-door
and sitting there doing what had to be
done – I very inconveniently,
experienced a muscle spasm. My left leg
and foot was now suddenly jammed up
against the door, and extremely rigid.
"What the hell was I going to do now?"
My bloomin' leg and foot just would not
budge!!

"Are you alright Alison?" A female member of the cabin crew said that. A queue must have been building up outside!! The captain had also just said, "Good morning Ladies and Gentlemen - we will be landing in Auckland in just over thirty minutes - I'll shortly be starting our descent." I felt bad for ignoring the member of cabin crew, at her second and third time of asking - I was now really concentrating on freeing both my foot and leg. To finally sit back in my seat was an enormous relief, in more ways than one!!!

Touching down at Auckland International Airport gave me an unbelievable feeling of self-satisfaction - 25 years older, and with my Emma - I found myself once again in New Zealand. I later learnt that Pete had recorded on video - our plane coming into land!!!

Very much to my surprise, I managed to maintain my composure on first catching sight of both Pete and Lisa and their children. I wasn't at all jet-lagged either.

JAMES OLIVIA AND CAITLIN

Prior to travelling from Auckland to Wellington, it was good just to relax and spend time with Emma, Pete and Lisa, and my nephew/nieces.

ALISON NEAR THE BEACH

With Pete and Lisa's black Labrador Jet safely in the local kennel – two cars packed up with a wheelchair, walking frame, twin buggy etc., etc. – it was now time for Pete, Lisa, Caitlin, James, Olivia, Emma and I to begin our ten hour drive to Wellington – the day being Wednesday 15th August.

Throughout the journey I found the scenery absolutely spectacular – I also couldn't get over how little traffic there is on the roads compared to England. We broke our journey on several occasions, and lunch was eaten in Taupo.

Arriving in Wellington – after first finding a suitable hotel for me, my excitement had now reached its peak. In the next few minutes I would finally be

reunited with my dear Nana and several
other relatives – some who last saw me
when I was only a baby!!

To see Nana with a huge smile on her
face, and waving at me when I arrived at
Bruce and Jill's house that evening made
it all worthwhile – I was so happy to
see her. Within minutes of my arrival,
poor Nana was briefly overcome with
emotion – to such a degree that she had
problems communicating, but thankfully,
she was absolutely fine.

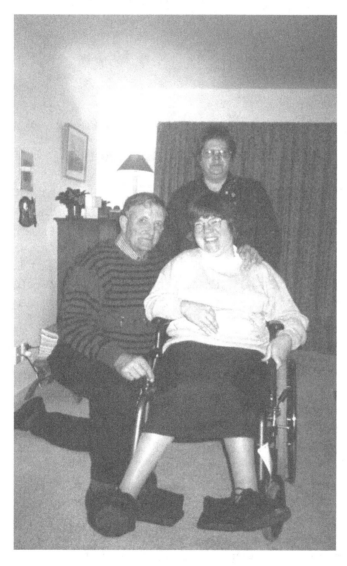

JANET RAY AND ALISON

A HUGE FAMILY REUION

CENTRAL CITY HOTEL

Our relatives certainly knew how to
play the game of hospitality and
entertainment, throughout the whole of
our holiday in New Zealand.
Unsurprisingly, Emma and I both had an
extremely enjoyable and memorable time.

**JILL AND ALISON OUTSIDE A
MAORI MEETING HOUSE
WITHIN THE TE PAPA MUSEUM**

**PETE ALISON AND BRUCE
ON THE QUAYSIDE**

**INDOOR ROCK CLIMBING
FOR EMMA AND NATALIE**

**JILL ALISON NANA DAVID
HELEN AND BRUCE**

Pete was very keen to grab an opportunity to show me the South Island, as I had never actually seen it before. So, on the morning of Friday 17th August, Pete, Emma, Bruce, Natalie and I boarded a ferry for a three hour sailing on the Cook Strait to Picton.

That sailing from north to south
was by no means smooth!! My wheelchair
joined the ship in rolling around, and
Emma had to ask the 'sick-bag-lady' for
assistance!!!

A hire-car was collected on our
arrival in Picton, and we soon found our
way to Nelson – where we booked
ourselves into a ground floor apartment,
before having a meal in a local
restaurant in the evening.

A VIEW OF NELSON

Every day during our holiday in New Zealand proved to be an eventful one – Saturday, 18th August was certainly no exception!!

Our stay in the South Island was originally, only supposed to be for 24 hours, but due to the rapid deterioration that had taken place with the weather overnight, we were forced to extend our stay by a further 24 hours. All ferry crossings had been cancelled – getting ourselves marooned could only happen to us!!!

In a crisis, it isn't what you know – it's who, you know!! On learning about our quandary, our relatives, Mary and Janet, were more than happy to come to our rescue. Meeting us in Blenheim we were later directed to Mary's Guest House in Kaikoura – where Mary provided us all with a much welcomed hot meal, a very comfortable bed for the night – followed by a very nice breakfast in the morning. "Thank you so much Mary – your company and hospitality is to be highly praised. Thanks a lot for your help too, Janet."

PHOTO COURTESY OF MARY WAREHAM

"A STAY AT 'WAREHAM HOUSE'
IS HIGHLY RECOMMENDED!!"

JANET AND ALISON
ADMIRING THE VIEW FROM MARY'S HOUSE

With the weather conditions much improved, it was now time to say our farewells to Mary and Janet, and make tracks back towards Picton, knowing that the ferry would be sailing on much calmer waters today – Sunday 19th August.

AN UNCLE AND NIECE HUG FOR ALISON AND BRUCE – IN NATIVE BUSH!!

"THEY'RE MY CARDS!!" An incensed woman – a fellow passenger suddenly shouted those words at Pete several times!! Poor Pete thought the cards

were for general use!! That obviously
put a rapid end to a couple of card
games with Emma and I. Fortunately, our
sailing back to Wellington didn't entail
anything more dramatic than that!!

BRUCE AND ALISON ABOARD THE FERRY

Monday, 20th August was scheduled to
be our last day in Wellington. Emma and
Natalie spent the day together at
school. I spent the morning at Helen and
David's house – and the afternoon with
Nana at Shona McFarlane Retirement
Village – a lovely place, for an equally
lovely lady.

I didn't want our time in Wellington
to end as it inevitably meant saying an
emotional goodbye – especially to Nana.
Hitting the rum and coke bottle with
Nana meant a really good laugh though!!

A CHILLY VIEW!!!

CAITLIN

CAITLIN PETE JAMES AND OLIVIA
"PLENTY OF SNOW IN AUGUST!!!"

"HERE EVERYONE COMES"
SAYS ALISON AND PETE

**EMMA JAMES OLIVIA
ALISON JET AND CAITLIN IN AUCKLAND**

Pete's enthusiasm to show Emma and I as much as possible never seemed to diminish.

Returning to 18 Anarahi Place and Carlson School was extremely strange for me.

**EMMA AND CAITLIN AT
18 ANARAHI PLACE**

ALISON AT CARLSON SCHOOL!!

The Auckland Sky Tower is most
definitely worth a visit - that is if
you've got a head for heights!!!

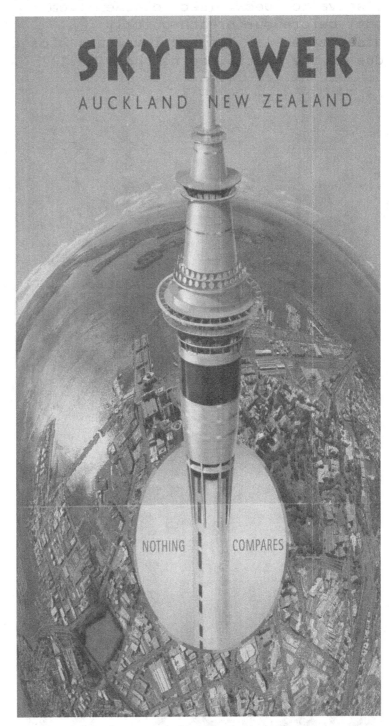

PHOTO COURTESY OF SKYCITY AUCKLAND SKY TOWER

For a matter of seconds Pete, Caitlin, Emma and I went out on the Observation Deck, (second level from top) before our breath quickly disappeared!!! The top level was closed due to the weather being too windy!!!

EMMA AND CAITLIN STANDING ON GLASS!!!

Still hungry for action and
adventure, Pete, Caitlin, Emma and I
were once again on the open road –
driving towards Rotorua. This of course
provided Pete and I with yet more
nostalgia!!

I was determined to not only see the
boiling mud pools, which Rotorua is
renowned for – but also a live Kiwi
bird, albeit, behind glass. Regrettably
we weren't able to stay long enough to
see any Maori's doing the Haka!!!

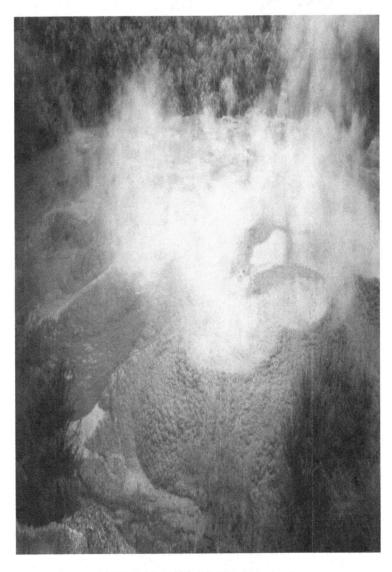

BOILING MUD POOL

CAITLIN PETE AND ALISON

**EMMA ALISON AND CAITLIN
OUTSIDE MAORI MEETING HOUSES**

Through our stomachs screaming at us
for food, it was obviously now time for
lunch! With Emma and Caitlin in one
Gondola, and Pete, my wheelchair and I
in another (only just!!), we all soon
found ourselves approaching a Sky-
Restaurant at relatively high-speed!!!

A GONDOLA VIEW OF ROTORUA

What did my Emma eat for her lunch?!! Without a doubt, it gave her a huge appetite for thrills – and thankfully, no, spills!!! One ride on a Sky-Swing wasn't satisfying enough for Emma. She had to scare the living daylights out of her mother – not once, but twice – a second time totally on her own!! As I witnessed my daughter swinging through the air, I kept thinking, "That's my baby!!!"

PREPARING

"READY, STEADY"

"GO!!!!"

"BYE.EEEEEEEE!!!!!"

"NOT VERY TALL!!!!"

On Saturday 25th August, with less
than 24 hours to go before boarding the
plane for our return flight back to
England, Emma was still craving for
action and height!! So, Pete and I
spent that afternoon watching our
niece/daughter going round and round,
and up and down on a roller-coaster at
Rainbows End in Auckland - numerous
times over!!!

On our way to Auckland International
Airport on Sunday 26th August, Pete
continued to provide me with a nostalgic
sightseeing tour. He couldn't let me
leave New Zealand without showing me
Middlemore Hospital. I can remember
taking my soft toy Winnie-the-Pooh Bear
to the operating theatre there, certain
that he would be having an operation
too!! I was only about seven years old
at the time.

Unavoidably, saying goodbye to Pete
and his family made my eyes change
colour! On arriving back at London
Heathrow on Monday 27th August, I was
feeling very satisfied and pleased with
myself. Suffering from severe jet lag
didn't bother me at all - I had achieved
my highest goal yet. "A promise made -
a promise kept!!!"

EPILOGUE

"One Door Closes -
Another One Opens"

The uncertainty relating to my job within Barclays Bank PLC came to an end officially on Friday, 9th May 2002. Immense effort to secure new employment following my redundancy has to date, proved to be very disappointing - that disappointment has taught me an awful lot about life though.

On Saturday 29th June 2002, just 10 months after rewarding my dear Nana with my long-term promise - she died. I personally will always be happy that she passed away a very contented lady. Sadness was thankfully soon replaced with happiness. On Friday 5th July 2002, I attended the wedding of Julia and Chris. A very special occasion for two very special people.

As I now conclude writing this book, I would like to express my utmost gratitude to my much loved family and huge circle of friends. I apologise if I haven't personally mentioned you by name, but an enormous "thank you" goes out to all concerned. "Without each and every one of you, I would not be the person I am today."

2nd March 2004

Printed in the United States
By Bookmasters